LITERACY FOR SCHOOL IMPROVEMENT

VALUE ADDED FOR MALTA

CHARLES MIFSUD
ROWENA GRECH
Literacy Unit
University of Malta

and

DOUGAL HUTCHISON
JO MORRISON
PETER RUDD
JOHN HANSON
National Foundation for Educational Research
England

Published by Agenda for the
National Foundation for Educational Research, UK,
the Literacy Unit, University of Malta
and the Education Division, Malta.

Agenda, Miller House, Tarxien Road, Airport Way, Luqa, Malta.
Tel: (+356) 21664488 E-mail: info@millermalta.com

Typeset at Media Centre Publications
Printed at Media Centre, Blata l-Bajda

First published in 2004

ISBN: 99932 - 622 - 8 - 5

Table of Contents

List of Tables

SECTION THREE

List of Figures

SECTION THREE

The Project Team

Dr Charles Mifsud, Director, Literacy Unit, University of Malta and Project Leader;

Ms Rowena Grech, Research Officer, Literacy Unit, University of Malta and Project Researcher;

Dr Dougal Hutchison, Chief Statistician, National Foundation for Educational Research, Slough, England, and Statistical Advisor to the Project;

Ms Jo Morrison, Senior Statistician, National Foundation for Educational Research, Slough, England, and Statistical Advisor to the Project;

Dr Peter Rudd, Principal Research Officer, School Improvement, National Foundation for Educational Research, Slough, England, and Research Advisor to the Project;

Mr John Hanson, Head of Database Production Group, National Foundation for Educational Research, Slough, England, and Data Matcher of the Project.

Authors

CHARLES MIFSUD is Head of the Department of Arts and Languages at the University of Malta. He holds post-graduate degrees from the Universities of Cambridge and London. He directs the Literacy Unit which has conducted a number of National Literacy Surveys in Malta. His main research interests are in literacy development and language teaching.

ROWENA GRECH is the Research Officer of the Literacy Unit at the University of Malta. She holds a BA (Hons) in English and is currently reading for an MA in Sociolinguistics. For a number of years Ms Grech taught English as a Foreign Language to adults. She has also been involved in the organisation of a number of projects in sociolinguistic research.

DOUGAL HUTCHISON is Chief Statistician at the National Foundation for Educational Research in England and Wales. He was one of the first people in the UK to carry out a value added study. His research interests include multilevel modelling and the introduction of new statistical analysis methods.

JO MORRISON has worked at the NFER for over 6 years, having studied previously for a B.Sc. in Mathematics and Statistics and an M.Sc. in Probability and Statistics. She has been involved in a wide variety of work throughout this time, including conference presentations and training others. Project work has included the repeat of IEA's (International Association for the Evaluation of Educational Achievement) Third International Mathematics and Science Study (TIMSS-R), the analysis of the Optional Year 3, 4 and 5 tests and NFER's Value-Added Service to Secondary Schools (formerly QUASE).

PETER RUDD is a Principal Research Officer in the Department of Evaluation and Policy Studies at the NFER. He leads the Department's work on School Effectiveness and School Improvement. Current topics of interest include the future of teaching and learning, school partnership working and 'school diversity' policies and programmes.

JOHN HANSON is the Head of the Database Production Group at NFER. He is responsible for processing and cleaning all quantitative data collected for the large number of projects run by NFER each year. He has worked at NFER for over ten years, after completion of an MSc in Computing Science. As part of his work he has previously led a number of large data collection projects in England, including the tracking, over a three-year period, of approximately 600,000 individual pupils as they progressed through national testing at ages 7 and 11. He also has considerable experience of database management, being responsible for the maintenance of NFER's database of all schools in England, Scotland, Wales and Northern Ireland.

Acknowledgements

We wish to express our appreciation of the efforts of a wide range of people whose hard work and dedication have made this project what it is. Our thanks are due to the following:

- the Education Division and UNESCO (Malta) for sponsoring the studies;
- all the primary schools in Malta for having taken the time and organisation to administer both the Year 2 and the Year 5 studies, and for their efforts in helping us match pupils from Year 2 to Year 5;
- the pupils for having taken both sets of tests;
- all the test administrators;
- to those who assisted in organising the Year 2 or Year 5 Literacy Studies, in particular Professor Greg Brooks, University of Sheffield, UK and Ms Josephine Milton, Ms Marjes Zammit and Ms Entela Dimech Llanaj, University of Malta, Malta;
- Dr Denis Vincent, University of East London, UK, leader of the team which developed the (English) *Reading Progress Baseline Test* and who carried out the standardisations of the Maltese and English versions used in this survey;
- Ms Emma Scott and Ms Joana Lopes of the National Foundation for Educational Research, Slough, UK, for carefully reading and checking earlier versions of the Value Added Survey manuscript;

- Ms Sally Green of the National Foundation for Educational Research, Slough, UK, for her tireless efforts to ensure that everything was properly organised in the UK;

- Ms Catherine Vella for compiling the index for this publication.

Foreword

This publication represents a national effort to monitor educational standards in a small island state, which is also a member of the European Union. This has been achieved through a process spanning over six years, and has included two National Literacy Surveys held in 1999 and 2002 with the same cohort, a Value Added Study, consultations with schools and a number of intervention programmes. It represents also an extensive, collaborative effort, which has involved various stakeholders in the field of education.

The Maltese Islands (Malta and Gozo) are situated in the Mediterranean Sea. While small compared with other countries, they represent a lively and dynamic community with a long history and a rich culture. Their position and cultural heritage mean that they are ideally placed as a link between the European and Arabic worlds.

One considerable asset in Malta's future derives from the Island's bilingual population. Virtually without exception, the population speaks both Maltese and English fluently. It will be important to preserve and enhance this heritage. Malta's concern with the success of its education is evident in the conduct of the two National Literacy Surveys, the Year 2 survey conducted in 1999, and the Year 5 survey, conducted in 2002. The level of skill available locally is shown by the use of specially-created tests of Maltese reading ability for these studies.

An important analytical tool to help schools improve their performance is a value added study. This helps a school to assess the progress made by its pupils in comparison with other schools. As a first step, it enables a school to assess its overall performance in relation to other schools, and then to examine its strengths and weaknesses in more detail. There are, inevitably, differences in intake and circumstances between schools, but a value added analysis allows those concerned to compare schools on a like with like basis.

In Section One of this publication, we report the findings of the Year 5 literacy survey in Maltese and English, conducted in 2002. This survey was conducted as a follow-up to the Year 2 literacy survey (Mifsud et al., 2000), which was carried out in 1999 with the same cohort of children.

Section Two reports on the Value Added Study which matched pupils between the Year 2 and Year 5 literacy surveys. This study examines any significant differences in the progress made by pupils in different types of schools. It examines also which factors were related to differences in pupil progress from Year 2 to Year 5.

Section Three makes a case for using value added data for school improvement. It presents a model of a value added school report and the implications of this for schools that wish to review the progress of their children and engage in forward planning.

Note: In the Maltese schooling system, at primary level, there are state schools and both private church and private independent schools. Within the state sector there are three types of schools: Schools "A", "B" and "C". Schools belonging to type "A" are those that house the following classes – Kindergarten 1, Kindergarten 2, and Years 1 to 3, that is, children from 3 to 7 years of age. Schools of type "B" house Years 4 to 6, that is, children from 8 to 10 years of age. Schools of type "C" house children from Kindergarten 1 to Year 6, that is children from 3 to 10 years of age.

Section One

The National Survey of the Attainment of Year 5 Pupils

Introduction

The first ever National Literacy Survey in Malta (Mifsud et al., 2000) was conducted with all Maltese 7-year-olds in Maltese and English. This survey investigated how well 6-to 7-year olds in Malta can read, both in Maltese and in English. This was the subject of the National Literacy Survey in Malta, carried out in March 1999. Virtually every child in the country born in 1992 was tested in both Maltese and English, using equivalent parallel tests, and complete data were gathered on 4,554 children.

The main findings and recommendations from that study were as follows:

- The average score in both languages was quite high, and this bilingual and biliterate outcome was very positive.
- The tests clearly identified pupils with literacy difficulties, and these children should be given additional support.
- Girls achieved significantly higher scores than boys.
- Children who had less than two years of pre-school education had significantly lower average scores than those who had more pre-school education.
- Pupils who had Special Educational Needs and/or were receiving Complementary Education had significantly lower average scores than other pupils.
- Pupils whose mothers and/or fathers were better educated, and whose fathers had middle-class jobs or better, achieved significantly higher average scores than others.
- Pupils in Church and Private Independent schools achieved significantly higher average scores than pupils in state schools.
- Schools in the South-Eastern part of Malta had the highest average scores, while those in the Inner Harbour Region and in Gozo achieved the lowest average scores.

One of the main recommendations of this report was that the "survey could be the start of a thorough programme of assessment in different subjects and over time, for example by repeating this Year 2 survey after (say) four years, and/or by following up this cohort of children in about four years' time". In March 2002 the National Literacy Survey was repeated with the same cohort of pupils. This was in fact three years after the original study, rather than the four years, which would have marked the end of primary schooling for the vast majority of pupils, but it was felt that this would have posed an extra and undesirable burden upon schools already heavily engaged with pupils preparing for secondary school entry.

Scope

- The second National Literacy Survey in Malta was carried out in March 2002 as a follow-up to the first National Literacy Survey carried out in March 1999.
- Every Year 5 pupil in Malta took an English test and a Maltese test of literacy. The Year 5 English test was a member of the same set of tests as the Year 2 test, but appropriate for an older age group. The Year 5 Maltese test was a substantially parallel Maltese adaptation of the English test used.
- Of the 99 schools in Malta with Year 5 pupils, all participated. Information was supplied for a total of 5,466 pupils. After excluding those pupils without key variables, such as a test score, full information was available on 4,973 pupils for both Maltese and English.

Main Findings

- The difference in attainment between boys and girls was statistically significant. Girls achieved significantly higher average scores than boys in both languages.

- Generally, older pupils performed better than younger pupils.
- Pupils performed better in their first language, that is, pupils whose first language was Maltese performed better in the Maltese test than their English-speaking peers, while pupils who spoke English as their first language performed better in the English test.
- Pupils in church and independent schools achieved significantly higher average scores than pupils in state schools in English.
- Pupils attending schools in the Inner Harbour region had significantly lower average scores in both languages than pupils attending schools in all the other regions, even when allowance for the home background of the pupils had been made.

Implications

Although to a lesser extent than in 1999 (the average scores for both the English and Maltese tests were lower in 2002 than in 1999), the Year 5 pupils were making good progress in literacy in both Maltese and English, and this bilingual and biliterate outcome was a very positive finding. The standardisation of the test in both languages has the potential to provide a useful educational and research tool.

From the detailed findings, it is possible to draw up two profiles, of the Maltese children most and least likely to succeed:

- most likely: a girl, born in the earlier part of the year, from the South Eastern region for Maltese, and the Northern region for English, born of highly educated parents, attending a church or independent school for English;
- least likely: a boy from the Inner Harbour region, born in the latter part of the year, born of poorly educated parents, with father in a low-paid job or unemployed, attending a state school for English.

However, these profiles do not mean that pupils fitting the 'most likely to succeed' profile are to be regarded as not needing help or attention. On the other hand, teachers should not have low expectations of what children who fit the 'least likely to achieve' profile can achieve.

The Maltese education system is clearly doing a lot to overcome initial inequalities, both because there are schools and pupils who buck these trends, and because of the good overall standard of attainment.

However, in view of recent developments concerning boy/girl differences in attainment, it could be considered worrying for those concerned with education that the gap between boys and girls should be so large even at Year 5 level. The initial differences in attainment of literacy should level out with the right schooling.

Also worrying is the gap in literacy attainment in both languages between pupils attending schools in the Inner Harbour region and those attending schools in the other regions of the country.

Main Recommendations

- Children whose standardised score was below 70 in either language should be identified by their schools, so that intensive individual support can be given to any of these children who are not already receiving it.
- Gender differences in attainment: action is required to ensure that boys do not fall behind in this important life skill. Gender differences may be reduced or reversed in other subjects and these may need their own strategies.
- Differences between state schools and church and independent schools especially regarding the English language: a policy aim could be that a great effort is made to improve the level of English in state education.
- Regional differences need to be investigated.

- Where extra resources are put in to implement policies to reduce inequalities, careful evaluation will be essential to measure their impact.
- This follow-up survey is important because the pupils' and schools' progress can be measured by comparing results obtained in 1999 with those obtained in 2002.
- These National Literacy Surveys (1999, 2002) may be the start of a thorough programme of assessment in different subjects.

Chapter 1

Background

The Maltese Islands have two official languages. Maltese, a Semitic language, is the native tongue. English is used widely and is taught from early on at school. For Malta and Gozo, it is the Language of Wider Communication (LWC).

In primary schools, oracy skills in English are introduced early on alongside Maltese at the kindergarten level and the beginning of Year 1 (five- and six-year-olds) of formal schooling. Literacy skills in English are introduced later on in Year 1. In Year 2 (six- to seven-year-olds), further oracy and literacy work is carried out in both Maltese and English. Increasingly, as children move from primary to secondary and then into tertiary education, English gains in importance.

Literacy in both languages is therefore essential; hence the decision of the Ministry of Education and the Literacy Unit of the University of Malta to carry out the national survey of literacy attainment in March 1999. It was decided that the first national survey of educational performance undertaken in Malta should focus on the reading attainment of Year 2 pupils, in both Maltese and English (Mifsud et al., 2000). The present follow-up study, conducted in March 2002 on all Year 5 pupils, investigated also the pupils' literacy attainment in both Maltese and English.

Chapter 2

Aims

The objectives of this project were:

- to conduct a national survey of the literacy attainment in both Maltese and English of all Maltese Year 5 pupils in state, private church and private independent primary schools as a follow-up to the first National Literacy survey carried out in 1999 on the same cohort of pupils when they were in Year 2 (Mifsud et al., 2000)
- to produce literacy tests in both Maltese and English for Year 5 pupils
- to obtain raw and standardised scores on both versions of the test for Maltese Year 5 pupils
- to provide feedback to all schools regarding the pupils' levels of literacy in both Maltese and English at this level
- to investigate the relationship between the pupils' levels of literacy and background variables at pupil, home and school levels
- to analyse the data using multilevel modelling, which takes into account the hierarchical structure of the data at school and pupil level
- to provide information on the levels of attainment in literacy of Maltese Year 5 pupils for the benefit of all stakeholders in Maltese education: the pupils themselves, their parents and teachers, administrators and policy makers
- to encourage public debate on the implications of the results for educational and social policy in Malta
- to be able to compare results at pupil and school levels, obtained in 1999 and 2002 by the same cohort of pupils

- to be able to make international comparisons, especially since the test used had previously been standardised in the UK
- to be able to investigate the relation between pupil attainment and home background which has been thoroughly investigated in a UK context (Strand, 1997; Tymms et al., 1997; Strand, 1999; Thrupp, 2001; Strand, 2002; Hutchison, 2003), and to see whether these findings are replicated in the Malta situation where there are many similarities, and at the same time many differences with the situation in the UK.

Chapter 3

Survey Administration

3.1 Tests

One problem faced by those who would like to investigate literacy skills in the Maltese situation is the lack of availability of standardised tests. There have been some attempts to design and trial word reading tests in Maltese and English by Falzon (1972), and in Maltese by Bartolo (1988). For children in Year 1, there is also a Maltese-language version of Clay's *Concepts About Print Test* (Martinelli, 1996). For the Year 2 age range there is a Maltese literacy test, which is a parallel version of the *Reading Progress Baseline Test* designed for the 1999 National Literacy Survey (Mifsud et al., 2000). No appropriate tests were available locally to assess the literacy skills of Year 5 pupils in Maltese and English.

3.1.1 English

After inspection of and consultation on the range of available English-language tests, a standardised British test was chosen for assessing the pupils' level of attainment in English. The test selected was *Reading Progress Test 3* within the *Reading Progress Tests* series (Vincent, et al., 1996). This test is part of a series of seven standardised tests developed by the East London Assessment Group at the University of East London in England.

The test can be administered either to a whole class or to small groups of pupils and covers different aspects of literacy. The test contains 41 items in all, and is standardised (in Britain) for the age range 7 years 8 months to 9 years 2 months (7:08–9:02). The decision to use it with somewhat older Maltese children took account of the fact that for most Maltese children, English is a second language.

3.1.2 Maltese

A Maltese parallel version of *Reading Progress Test 3* was devised by a group of Maltese educators who are specialists in the Maltese language and have extensive teaching experience.

The Maltese test contained exactly the same number of items as the English version, and covered the same skills. The page layout, graphic style and typeface were identical to those in the English version.

3.1.3 A Brief Outline of the Maltese and English Tests

The test is divided into 8 sections. In the first section, which consists of four multiple-choice questions of the non-narrative, retrieval type, the pupils are expected to identify objects that can fly. This section tests the pupils' knowledge of vocabulary both in the question and the answer.

In the second section the pupils are asked to read a passage entitled "The Talking Garden" and to answer three questions by choosing the right picture. This exercise tests the pupils' comprehension, their narrative and inferential skills.

In the third part of the test, after reading the passage called "My Granddad", the pupils have to make assumptions on what they have just read, by hypothesising on who or what might have said a particular sentence from their knowledge of the text. Once again this section tests the pupils' narrative and inferential skills.

In the next section of the test, the pupils are asked to read a poem; "Mother parrot's advice to her children". This part of the test aims to assess the pupils' knowledge of specific items of vocabulary like 'never', and 'dispute', by replacing one item with another in the test item, and their narrative skills. For example, in the test item pupils need to know that 'dispute' is a synonym of 'argue'. Pupils are also tested on their knowledge of particular grammar items like the prefix 'un-' for the negative and modals like 'should'.

The next text in the reading broadsheet entitled "Parrots in Danger" is a factual text. It provides pupils with information on the different types of parrots and how they are being endangered by humans. There are two sections in the question booklet that test the pupils' comprehension of this text. The first is of the multiple-choice, non-narrative type, while the second section is a set of 'true', 'false', 'doesn't say' questions also of the non-narrative type. These two sections of the test require a higher level of knowledge of the text. Besides being tested on particular items of vocabulary, pupils are also tested on their understanding of syntax. To answer particular questions, pupils are expected to make coherence in two or more consecutive sentences. They are indirectly being tested on their knowledge of reference devices, in this case in an anaphoric manner. For example:

> "You will find most parrots in the trees of the rainforest, but some live in the mountains and some live on the ground. One of these..."

where "one of these" refers to "parrots" in the previous sentence. Question 21, that is the last question in this section, is an inferential question and requires students to review the whole text.

The next section, "A Talent For Talk" is a cloze procedure test. Pupils are expected to fill in the gaps with suitable words. This section of the test is the only section preceded by a practice test item, due to the level of difficulty of the exercise.

The final section of the test is a set of multiple-choice questions about all the four texts in the reading booklet. This section requires higher order reading skills, as pupils are required to review whole texts rather than specific parts. In addition to this, the last section assesses pupils' sensitivity to genre. For example, when asked about which text gives "... the most useful information for a project ..." the pupils are expected to know that this refers to the text entitled "Parrots in Danger", which is the only factual text included in this test.

3.1.4 Instruction Booklets

For the English version of the test, the original teacher's manual (Vincent et al., 1997) was used as the instruction booklet for test administrators. However, if the test administrators felt that the pupils did not understand all the instructions in English, they were free to explain in Maltese as well.

For the Maltese version of the test, the original teacher's manual was translated into Maltese and adapted according to the Maltese test items. The test administrators were free to explain in English if there were pupils who were unable to follow the instructions in Maltese.

3.2 Field Testing

Field testing of the reading attainment in Maltese and English of Maltese Year 5 pupils was carried out between March 2001 and June 2001 using the *Reading Progress Test 3* tests described above. In addition to this, a number of pupils of mixed ability were tested to assess their literacy level in English using *Reading Progress Test 4* and *Reading Progress Test 5*.

Background data were collected on the pupils and schools involved. The number of pupils tested using *Reading Progress Test 3* in both languages was 40. They were pupils born in 1991, of mixed ability, in Year 5, and belonged to 2 state primary schools, 1 private independent school and 1 private church school.

The test administrators' ratings showed a high level of approval of the tests. The average raw marks for *Reading Progress Test 3* in both languages was satisfactory in all 4 schools.

The same 40 pupils, from the same 4 schools as those for *Reading Progress Test 3*, were tested for their literacy attainment in English using *Reading Progress Test 4* and *Reading Progress Test 5*. The average marks for both tests were not satisfactory and it was decided to proceed with *Reading Progress Test 3* for the Year 5 National Literacy Survey, for both Maltese and English.

3.3 Other Research Instruments

The other research instruments used in the survey were intended to gather information about the schools, the Year 5 classes and the pupils involved.

3.3.1 School Questionnaire

A School Questionnaire was designed (see Annex I and II) which requested data at school level: the geographical region of the school, and the number of male and female pupils in Year 5. The Head or Assistant Head of School was asked to provide this information.

3.3.2 Pupil Data Form

A Pupil Data Form (see Annex III and IV) was designed. It requested information about a variety of pupil- and family-level background variables: age, gender, first language, father's occupation, mother's occupation, father's level of education, mother's level of education, special educational needs, and the name of the school the child attended in Year 2.

It was envisaged that the test administrators would be able to obtain most of the information from the Cumulative Record Card (CRC) that schools usually compile for every pupil. The CRC lists the pupil's name, surname, date of birth, father or guardian's name, mother's name, address, father's occupation, mother's occupation, and the pupil's personality and behaviour, physique and health, and school(s) attended. Space is also provided for other relevant information and for final reports by the Heads of School.

Additional information which does not feature in the CRC, such as mother's level of education and father's level of education, was obtained through the class teacher or complementary teacher with the help of the pupils' parents or primary carer(s).

3.3.3 Suitability and Manageability Questionnaire

The test administrators were asked to complete a short questionnaire (see Annex V) on the suitability of the tests for Year 5 pupils, and the manageability of the test administration.

3.4 Samples of Schools and Pupils

All 99 schools on the Maltese Islands with pupils in Year 5 were invited to take part. The sample included all Year 5 pupils in state, private church and private independent primary schools in Malta and Gozo (See Table 3.1 below); the total number of pupils on whom data were collected was 5,849 pupils (see Section 4.1).

According to the official definition, Year 5 children in the school year 2001/2002 were those born between 1st January 1992 and 31st December 1992, both dates inclusive. Therefore, pupils who were eligible by date of birth for inclusion in the survey, but who were repeating Year 4 or had been 'promoted' to Year 6, were included as they fell within the official age bracket. On the other hand, a small number of pupils who were in Year 5 classes, whose age was above the age range of Year

Table 3.1: Sample of Schools and Classes

Type of school	No. of schools
State schools	62
Private church schools	25
Private independent schools	12
Total	99

5 pupils, (as they were repeating the year) completed the tests. However, their scores were not used in the data analyses. There were also a few pupils who were in Year 5 classes and completed the tests but who were below the required age (i.e. they were born after 31st December 1992).

3.5 Test Administrators

The test administrators were complementary teachers, support teachers, Assistant Heads and Heads of School. Since these members of staff are not responsible for a particular class, they were able to attend the training seminar during school hours without disrupting the school schedule.

A training seminar was held on the 4th February 2002 and featured: an introduction to the aims and objectives of the study, the role of the test administrators, an introduction to the various research instruments they would be required to complete, and instructions for administering and marking the tests. There were opportunities for questions and feedback throughout. All the test administrators became familiar with all the research instruments and instructions as these were reviewed extensively. At the end of this seminar, they were provided with a pack including the School Questionnaire, Pupil Data Forms, tests and instruction booklets.

A follow-up meeting was held on 15th March 2002 so that the test administrators could provide feedback regarding the tests and return all tests and other research instruments to the Literacy Unit.

3.6 Data Collection

Each class was administered the Maltese and English tests. To reduce practice effects, the teachers were asked to administer the Maltese test first to the pupils who were listed as even numbers and the English test first to the pupils listed as odd numbers on the class register. Test administrators were to allow at least one day between the administration of the two versions of the test.

Pupils who were absent on one of the testing days were allowed to sit for the test if they returned to school the following day. The tests were designed so as to allow their administration to whole classes or large groups. The pupils were given a question booklet together with a reading broadsheet. The test administrator went through the question booklet explaining what was expected of the pupils in every section. The administrator of the test explained also which text the pupils had to read from the reading broadsheet in order to answer each set of questions in the question booklet. The pupils were then given approximately 45-50 minutes to complete each test. It was very important for the pupils to complete their answers without discussion, collaboration or copying. The test administrator encouraged the pupils to attempt all questions and explained that the answers should be indicated by clearly marking a choice. During the test, only feedback relating to the method of answering was allowed (for example, if more than one choice had been marked or if the pupil was at the wrong item).

3.7 Scoring the Tests

The test administrators were trained to score the tests according to the instructions in the original teacher's manual (English version; Vincent et al., 1997) and the adapted instructions booklet for the Maltese version. Each right answer was awarded one mark.

Before data entry, some tests were checked at random to ensure that the test administrators' marking was accurate, and the level of accuracy was found to be satisfactory. Moreover, both the individual item scores (right/wrong) and the total score as calculated by the marker were entered; computer calculation of the total score from the item scores provided a crosscheck on the marker's accuracy.

After data entry, three tests for each language from each Year 5 class were checked at item level against the original test booklets. If any errors were encountered, a thorough check of all the question booklets of that class was carried out.

Chapter 4

Data Analysis

The first part of this section provides information about the size of the achieved sample and some technical data on the reliability of the tests. The rest of the section reports on how the statistical analyses of the test results were carried out. The use of multilevel modelling and the standardisation of the tests are described.

4.1 The Achieved Samples

The tests were administered in March 2002 in 252 classes containing Year 5 pupils in 99 schools. Data were gathered on 5,849 pupils. Finally, a total of 4,933 pupils were included for data analysis. The rest were either not eligible to participate as they were outside the required age range, which for Year 5 pupils at the date of testing was 9 years 2 months to 10 years 1 month (9:02–10:01), or they had missing data.

4.2 Suitability and Manageability

The 99 test administrators were asked to complete a suitability and manageability questionnaire. Eighty-one of the 99 test administrators completed the questionnaire. The suitability of the tests referred to the pupils' level and ability. The manageability of the tests dealt with whether the test administrators felt the tests were manageable to administer to the pupils. The majority of test administrators felt that both the Maltese and English tests were manageable. However, most test administrators did not consider the tests very suitable. The Maltese test was considered mostly 'fairly suitable', while the English test was thought to be 'borderline' (see Tables 4.1 and 4.2).

Table 4.1: Suitability Ratings (N=81)

	Maltese	English
Very suitable	13	9
Fairly suitable	46	27
Borderline	19	35
Unsuitable	3	10

Table 4.2: Manageability Ratings (N=81)

	Maltese	English
Very manageable	51	45
Fairly manageable	28	26
Borderline	2	9
Unmanageable	0	1

4.3 Reliability

The reliability of the tests was estimated in two ways: the correlation between the two versions, and their internal reliability. The tests were administered in counterbalanced order (half of the pupils took Maltese first, while half took English first).

The correlation between the two tests for all schools was high: on Pearson's Product-moment coefficient of linear correlation, r = 0.75. Figure 4.1 illustrates the correlation.

Cronbach's standardised alpha computed from correlations also indicated clearly that both the Maltese (alpha = 0.8540) and English (alpha = 0.8641) versions of the test had high internal reliability.

4.4 Raw Scores

The immediate output of the statistical analyses was average raw scores. In themselves, these provided only one useful finding, the high level of overall attainment in the two languages (see Section

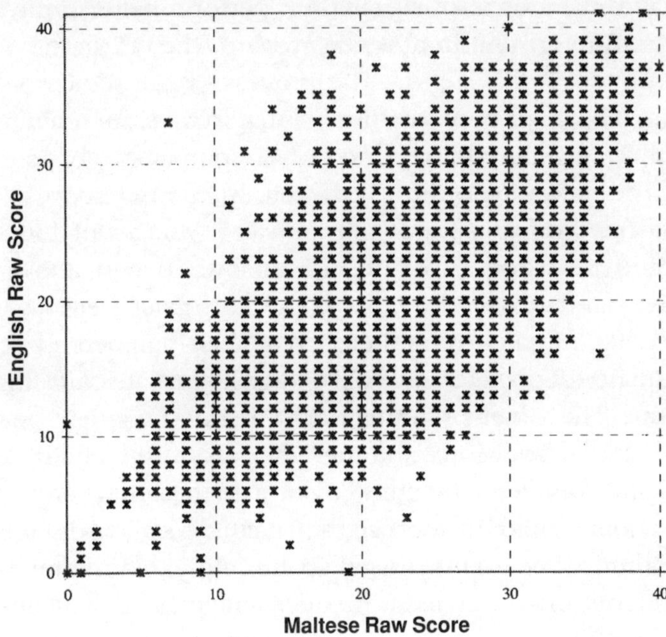

Figure 4.1: Correlation between Maltese and English tests.

5.1). More importantly, the raw scores served as input to the calculation of standardised scores, and to multilevel modelling.

4.5 Standardised Scores

An age-standardisation on a British sample already existed for *Reading Progress Test 3* (Vincent et al., 1996). However, English is usually a second language for Maltese pupils. For this reason a separate age-standardisation of the English test was carried out on the Maltese sample. The Maltese test was age-standardised with the same pupils. Both standardisations were performed by Dr Denis Vincent of the University of East London in England. Thus there now exist parallel standardised Maltese and English literacy tests for Maltese Year 5 children.

As is well known, older children perform better on average than younger children, even within the 12-month span represented in this survey. The process of age-standardisation aims to take account of this so that scores for children of different ages may be reported on a comparable basis.

In the standardisation process, the raw scores were transformed on to a scale with a mean (average) of 100 and a standard deviation (s.d.) of +15. Below 70 and above 130, precise standardised scores are not usually given because of the inaccuracy of calculating them from small numbers of scores.

Standardisation takes each child's age at the date of testing into account. The tables of norms form a matrix, in which one axis is the child's raw score, and the other axis is the child's age in years and completed months. Looking up the cell where the two facts about a child intersect gives that child's standardised score.

Children whose standardised scores fall within the range 85–115 can be considered in the broad 'average' band of attainment. Those between 116 and 130 are bright, and those above 130 gifted. Those between 70 and 84 are likely to be struggling with literacy, and therefore probably with the whole of their education, and require support; and those below 70 are severely disabled for learning and require very special attention.

It would be pointless to reproduce the distributions of standardised scores because by definition they would be identical for both languages – the standard normal or Gaussian distribution, perhaps better known as the 'bell curve'. For the same reason no findings based on the standardised scores are reported, since they would merely replicate the standard facts about the standard distribution. But the standardised tests have the potential to serve as very useful educational and research tools.

4.6 Multilevel Modelling

In education, as in many other areas of research, data occur in a structured arrangement. Schools contain classes, which in turn are made up of pupils. In general it occurs that there is a degree of similarity between the lower-level elements within a higher-level element. Thus, pupils within a school will be more similar to each other than they will be to pupils chosen at random from the entire population of schools and pupils. This hierarchical quality is not acknowledged in the standard 'traditional' statistical techniques, but the technique of **multilevel modelling** (Raudenbush and Bryk, 2002; Goldstein, 2003) has been developed precisely to take account of hierarchical structures. This is the technique used here. MLwiN is the multilevel programme used in this study (Rasbash et al., 2000).

When trying to investigate the effects of different school types on pupil progress, it was important to take into account a large number of possible confounding factors which may confuse the issue. For example, it is clear from a number of other studies that pupil characteristics, such as gender, parental education and occupation, and first language, were likely to be relevant, so information on all of these was collected at each sweep.

In order to explore the relationships between some measurable outcome and numerous factors that potentially affect it, a statistical technique called '*regression*' should be employed. This allows us to measure the extent to which each of the pupil, home and school factors that have been collected influences pupils' scores on tests of literacy. A particular form of regression analysis, called '*multilevel modelling*', allows us to take account of the fact that the cases are grouped. For example in this study pupils are grouped within schools. It is important to incorporate this information into any statistical analysis because it is likely that units that are grouped together will be more similar to each other than they are to units in different groups. In this case, because schools differ and pupils who attend the same school are exposed to the same school-level influences e.g. teaching styles, ethos, physical environment, etc., they are more likely to be similar to each other than they are to pupils who attend other schools.

An analysis which looks only at school-level data is less useful than the multilevel approach used in this research, because the latter can 'average out' important differences between different types of school and the way in which individual pupils progress. Ignoring such differences can give misleading results (see Schagen & Goldstein, 2002). The work done here is consistent with a range of other analyses carried out recently by the National Foundation for Educational Research (NFER), UK, which looked at the impact of different types of schools on value added performance measures (see e.g. Hutchison, 1993, 2003, Schagen & Morrison, 1998).

Two levels are considered here: school and pupil. Other levels of grouping are possible, such as classes within schools. However, school and pupil are considered to be the two most important here: a substantial proportion (slightly over 25 per cent) of Maltese primary schools have only one Year 5 class, so that for them school and class effects would not be separately identifiable.

Table 4.3 shows the background variables used in the multilevel modelling analyses, with their subcategories. These factors were considered first singly, then together.

Two parallel multilevel analyses were carried out, one for Maltese, the other for English. The outcome variable in each of these was the raw score. Two different multilevel models were employed. Firstly each of the variables were included in the model individually. This allowed us to determine the impact of each of the factors separately. This is known as the '*unadjusted*' model. The second model included all the variables together so that each variable is considered simultaneously with all the other factors that may affect pupil performance. This is referred to as the '*adjusted*' model.

Table 4.3: Background Variables Used in Multilevel Modelling, with Subcategories

Pupil variables	Subcategories
Gender	Male Female
Age	Up to 9 years 7 months at date of testing* Over 9 years 7 months at date of testing*
First Language	Maltese (including Maltese and other) English (including English and other) Other (including bilingual with no predominant language)
Special Educational Needs	None Mild to moderate Severe to very severe
Home variables	
Mother's Education	No formal schooling Primary school Secondary school Pre-university courses and vocational courses Tertiary education Other
Father's Education	No formal schooling Primary school Secondary school Pre-university courses and vocational courses Tertiary education Other
Mother's Occupation	Professional Managerial and administrative Higher clerical, skilled craftsmen, technicians Skilled manual workers, foremen Semi-skilled, unskilled workers, labourers Other
Father's Occupation	Professional Managerial and administrative Higher clerical, skilled craftsmen, technicians Skilled manual workers, foremen Semi-skilled, unskilled workers, labourers Other

Table 4.3: Background Variables Used in Multilevel Modelling, with Subcategories (continued)

Pupil variables	Subcategories
School variables	
Number of Year 5 classes in the School	1 – 7, 9
Type of School	Primary B State School Primary C State School Private Independent School Private Church School
Region of the School	Inner Harbour Outer Harbour South Eastern Western Northern Gozo

*Date of testing: March 2002

Note 1: 'State B' schools are primary schools which contain Years 4 to 6, and 'State C' schools are primary schools which contain kindergarten and Years 1 to 6.

Note 2: The father's and mother's occupation categories are adapted from Vassallo et al. (1994) (See Annex III).

The results arising from the use of these models are given below. Detailed results (tabulations of the coefficients, standard errors and tests of significance) for both the unadjusted and adjusted models are provided after the summary results, in tables 6.1 and 6.2.

Chapter 5

Findings: Raw Scores

5.1 Results for the Maltese Test

The maximum possible score on the Maltese test was 41. Raw scores achieved by pupils ranged from 0 to 41. The graph below shows the distribution of their scores.

Figure 5.1 shows that the distribution is slightly skewed towards a higher score. The mean score on the Maltese test was 24.39 (with a standard deviation of 6.7) and the median score was 25. The mean and the median raw scores are similar and are both greater than half of the maximum marks available.

The reliability of a test is a measure of the extent to which a pupil's test scores would vary with repeated testing, assuming that there was no fatigue, learning or lack of motivation. The

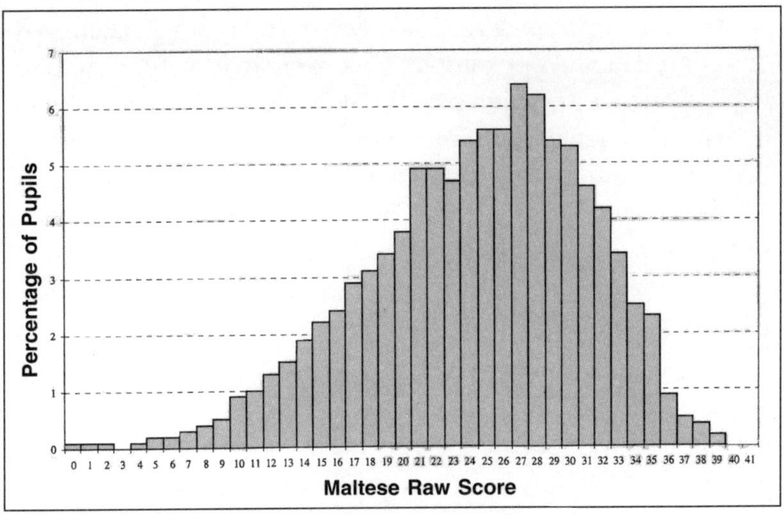

Figure 5.1: Frequency distribution of raw scores on the Maltese test.

more consistent the scores, the higher the reliability. Cronbach's Alpha is a measure of the reliability of a test. Cronbach's alpha for the Maltese test was 0.8540. For a test of literacy this value of reliability is acceptable.

Table 5.1 below presents the average raw scores of boys and girls on the Maltese test.

On average the girls scored just over 1 mark more than the boys on the Maltese test. This difference in performance was also seen in the first National Literacy Survey in 1999 and is the usual pattern in other formal education systems. When looking at the international scene, girls seem to achieve slightly higher scores than their male counterparts when it comes to literacy. The 2001 IEA study of Progress in International Reading Literacy (Mullis et al., 2003) found, for pupils of 9 years to 9 years 11 months, that girls were ahead in reading literacy in all 27 countries surveyed, though only about three quarters of these were statistically significant.

However, it should be noted that differences in performance between boys and girls may be due to other factors not considered here. For example, if we were to look for differences in performance between pupils who resided in different regions of Malta and neglected to incorporate other information, it could be that any differences found were associated with those pupils having higher levels of SEN or more highly paid parents. In order to investigate differences in performance rigorously, all factors need to be taken into consideration. The multilevel models presented later in this report address this.

Table 5.1: Boys' and Girls' Raw Scores on the Maltese Test

	No. of Pupils	Mean Raw Score	S.d.
Boys	2507	23.68	6.97
Girls	2426	25.11	6.36
Total	4933	24.39	6.72

5.2 Results for the English Test

The English test had a maximum possible score of 41. Pupils obtained scores ranging between 0 and 41. The graph below shows the distribution of their scores.

The mean score on the English test was 22.03 (the standard deviation was 7.1) and the median score was 22. These scores were lower than those for the Maltese test. As shown in Figure 5.2, the distribution of English scores is symmetrical showing that, unlike the Maltese test, the majority of pupils obtained raw scores in the middle of the score range.

The measure of reliability, Cronbach's Alpha, for the English test was 0.8641. For a test of literacy this value of reliability is acceptable.

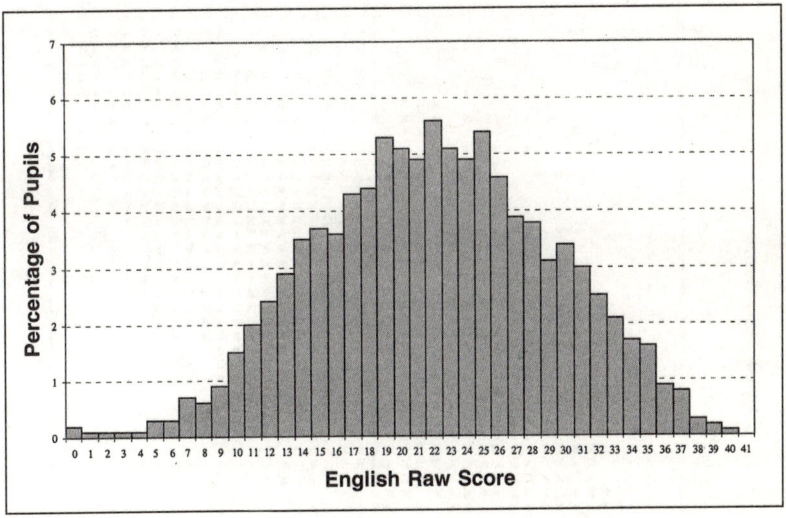

Figure 5.2: Frequency distribution of raw scores on the English test.

Table 5.2 below shows the average raw scores of boys and girls on the English test.

Again the girls' average raw score was higher than the boys',

Table 5.2: Boys' and Girls' Raw Scores on the English Test

	No. of Pupils	Mean Raw Score	S.d.
Boys	2507	21.45	7.29
Girls	2426	22.63	6.86
Total	4933	22.03	7.10

by about 1 mark. This scale of difference in performance was also seen in the first National Literacy Survey in 1999.

However, as stated earlier, in order to investigate differences in performance thoroughly it is important to consider as far as

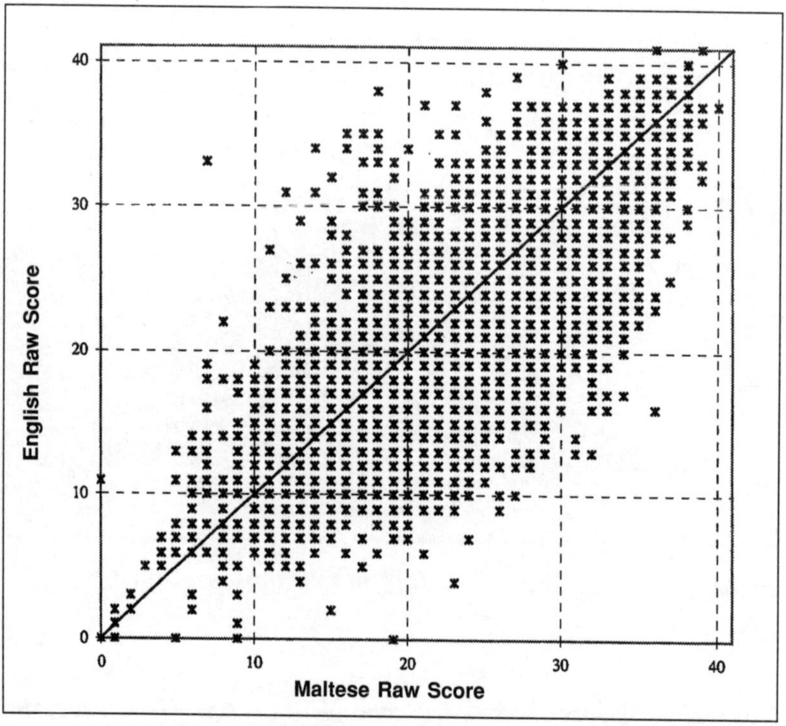

Figure 5.3: The relationship between raw scores on the English and the Maltese tests.

possible all other factors simultaneously. This was addressed through multilevel modelling (see Chapter 6).

Pupils' scores on the two tests were plotted on a graph. Figure 5.3 shows the relationship between the two test scores. Individual pupils are represented by an x.

The graph shows that as pupils' scores on one test increase, their scores on the other test tend to increase. This graph of the two test scores, along with the correlation of 0.752, shows that there is a fairly strong positive relationship between the scores on the two tests.

In order to look at pupils' relative performances on both tests it is useful to consider the line representing equal scores on the Maltese and English tests. It can be seen that there are more points on the graph below the line than above it. This indicates that pupils tended to score more highly on the Maltese test than they did on the English test. This reflects what has already been reported in the score distributions of the two tests, and is not unexpected considering that the majority of pupils' first language was Maltese.

Chapter 6

Findings: Multilevel Modelling

In this section, the results of the multilevel analyses are described, starting with the Maltese results, followed by the English results.

6.1 Maltese

Table 6.1 shows the results of the multilevel analyses, first with all the variables taken singly ('unadjusted'), and then including all variables simultaneously ('adjusted'). The aim of this sort of analysis is to estimate the differences between the subgroups when as many of the other potential influences as possible are taken into account. Thus, if we found that one region of the island scored more highly than another, it might be less an effect of the schools in that area than because it was a wealthier area, and more of the parents were highly educated.

The interpretation of one section of Table 6.1, namely the gender effect, will be described in some detail below to facilitate the interpretation of the rest of the variables.

Pupil Variables

6.1.1 Gender

The column labelled *N* gives the numbers of girls and boys. Differences in attainment between the categories, here between boys and girls, are described by setting the results for one 'base' group (here boys) equal to zero, and then expressing scores for other groups as differences from this base group. The unadjusted difference in attainment between girls and boys was 1.19, much larger than the standard error of this difference (0.20), suggesting that the difference was statistically significant. It is generally recommended that a better means of assessing statistical

Table 6.1: Unadjusted and Adjusted Results: Maltese

			Unadjusted model			Adjusted model		
		N	Coefficient	s.e.	Chi-square	Coefficient	s.e.	Chi-square
Pupil variables								
Gender	Boys	2542	0	–	37.4***	0	–	29.8***
	Girls	2431	1.19	0.195		0.97	0.177	
Age	In years and (completed) months	4973	0.15	0.025	36.5***	0.13	0.023	31.4***
First language	Maltese	4586	0	–	19.9***	0	–	54.8***
	English	357	-1.61	0.424		-2.72	0.394	
	Other (inc. bilingual)	30	-2.96	1.168		-3.48	1.068	
SEN	None	4752	0	–	402.4***	0	–	328.5***
	Mild to moderate	157	-8.37	0.519		-7.19	0.498	
	Severe to very severe	64	-10.59	0.798		-9.19	0.758	
Home variables								
Mother's Education	Other	191	0	–	260.7***	0	–	48.7***
	No formal schooling	15	1.23	1.661		0.10	1.752	
	Primary School	414	0.32	0.596		-1.07	0.659	
	Secondary School	3470	3.88	0.512		1.04	0.584	
	Pre-university courses and vocational courses	504	5.65	0.571		1.90	0.641	
	Tertiary Education	379	6.09	0.591		1.97	0.683	
Father's Education	Other	286	0	–	292.9***	0	–	34.7***
	No formal schooling	22	1.95	1.363		1.05	1.452	
	Primary School	511	2.11	0.482		1.74	0.579	
	Secondary School	2978	4.32	0.407		2.21	0.521	
	Pre-university courses and vocational courses	507	6.06	0.481		2.96	0.587	
	Tertiary Education	669	6.71	0.461		3.24	0.596	

Table 6.1: Unadjusted and Adjusted Results: Maltese (continued)

			Unadjusted model			Adjusted model		
		N	Coefficient	s.e.	Chi-square	Coefficient	s.e.	Chi-square
Mother's Occupation	Other	3694	0	–	92.2***	0	–	21.5***
	Professional	261	2.67	0.408		0.87	0.445	
	Managerial and administrative	164	0.59	0.514		-0.50	0.490	
	Higher clerical, skilled craftsmen, technicians	372	2.23	0.345		1.03	0.331	
	Skilled manual workers and foremen	160	0.69	0.506		0.45	0.467	
	Semi-skilled, unskilled workers, labourers	322	-1.18	0.372		-0.79	0.343	
Father's Occupation	Other	443	0	–	301.2***	0	–	74.3***
	Professional	411	5.86	0.440		2.42	0.514	
	Managerial and administrative	837	4.92	0.379		2.28	0.412	
	Higher clerical, skilled craftsmen, technicians	848	4.78	0.367		2.12	0.394	
	Skilled manual workers and foremen	1471	2.77	0.338		0.79	0.363	
	Semi-skilled, unskilled workers, labourers	963	1.79	0.356		0.17	0.376	

School variables								
No. Year 5 classes	1	531	0	–	7.9	0	–	16.9**
	2	1301	0.03	0.699		0.10	0.476	
	3	1034	-1.30	0.825		-1.47	0.551	
	4	811	-1.26	0.922		-1.01	0.689	
	5	808	-1.94	1.020		-2.50	0.898	
	6	124	-1.74	2.493		-1.68	1.642	
	7	166	-2.07	2.477		0.10	1.629	
	9	198	-1.10	2.469		-2.51	1.765	
Type of School	Primary B State School	1588	0	–	22.9***	0	–	23.4***
	Primary C State School	1529	0.39	0.669		-0.63	0.732	
	Private Independent School	598	2.38	0.886		0.65	0.773	
	Private Church School	1258	2.95	0.731		1.65	0.776	
Region	Inner Harbour	1290	0	–	11.3**	0	–	29.7***
	Outer Harbour	1437	1.56	0.721		2.14	0.531	
	South Eastern	612	2.31	0.879		3.02	0.616	
	Western	672	1.95	0.871		2.05	0.579	
	Northern	572	1.21	1.007		2.50	0.749	
	Gozo	390	2.07	0.847		1.79	0.585	
State schools only								
Region	Inner Harbour	411	0	–	35.1***	0	–	21.2***
	Outer Harbour	966	3.06	0.68		2.58	0.69	
	South Eastern	564	4.47	0.73		3.08	0.68	
	Western	473	3.70	0.78		1.91	0.70	
	Northern	417	3.79	0.85		2.31	0.83	
	Gozo	286	4.06	0.79		2.31	0.70	

significance is by means of the deviance, and by comparing the deviance of the relevant groups by using the statistical test known as 'chi-squared'. Here the chi-squared value was 37.4, which was statistically significant at the .001 level (indicated by the three asterisks), i.e. very highly significant. The columns for 'adjusted' results give the result after allowing for all the other factors. The difference was smaller, but still very highly statistically significant (chi-squared = 29.8, $p < .001$).

We can gain an impression of the size of these effects by comparing them with the population standard deviation (6.6). The effect of 1.19 means that the standardised difference between boys and girls is 1.19/6.6, i.e. of the order of 20 percent.

6.1.2 Age

Older pupils performed significantly better than younger pupils. The coefficient here means the effect of being one month older. There is a coefficient of 0.15, which means that for every month older, on average a child will score 0.15 points more, that is, a child of 9 years 5 months will score 0.15 points more than a child of 9 years 4 months.

6.1.3 First Language

Pupils who did not speak Maltese as their first language performed less well than those who did. Pupils who spoke other languages (which included bilingual children) achieved about 3 marks fewer than native Maltese speaking pupils. Pupils who spoke English as their first language obtained, on average, just over 1.6 marks fewer than their Maltese speaking peers. However this dropped to about 3.5 marks when all other variables were taken into account.

6.1.4 Special Educational Needs

Special educational needs on average had the most effect on pupils' raw score. Pupils with mild to moderate levels of

Special Educational Needs scored about 7 or 8 points lower than pupils without any SEN. Pupils with severe to very severe levels of SEN obtained raw scores of about 9 or 10 points lower. Many, though not all, pupils who were classified as having Special Educational Needs had learning difficulties. Even after adjusting for other factors, pupils with mild to moderate SEN obtained about 7 points lower, while those with severe to very severe SEN obtained about 9 points lower than pupils with no SEN.

Home Variables

6.1.5 Mother's Education

Pupils whose mothers were educated to at least secondary school level achieved higher raw scores than pupils whose mothers had lower levels of education. Their average raw scores ranged from 4 to 6 marks more and rose with the level of their mother's education. This difference in marks dropped to 1 or 2 marks when all other variables were taken into account.

6.1.6 Father's Education

The same relationship existed with the father's level of education except that after allowing for other factors, pupils whose fathers were educated to primary school level or above achieved higher raw scores than pupils whose fathers either had no formal schooling or were categorised as 'Other' (father's level of education was not known, father was not present in child's life or was deceased).

6.1.7 Parental Occupation

The mothers' occupations were significantly related to their children's raw score, but the effects became substantially smaller after allowing for other factors.

The fathers' occupations significantly impacted on their children's raw score and followed the ordering of the classification itself, though again these effects became smaller after allowing for other factors. The mother's occupation appeared to have a smaller effect than the father's. This was not surprising because most mothers fell into the group labelled 'Other' (presumably homemakers), which was used as a baseline. The mother's occupation seemed to have the lowest effect of the parental education and occupation groupings both before and after taking the other factors into account. However, this effect was still substantial.

School Variables

6.1.8 Number of Year 5 Classes

Some differences in raw scores were detected depending on the number of Year 5 classes in the school. Mainly pupils in schools with 3 or more classes got slightly lower score points than pupils in schools with 1 or 2 classes. However there was no statistically significant pattern to this differential performance.

6.1.9 Type of School

Pupils who attended independent and church schools performed better than those who attended state schools, by about 2 or 3 marks. Differences dropped significantly after taking other factors into account.

6.1.10 Region

Pupils in different regions of Malta performed differentially. Even after adjusting for other factors, pupils from most regions achieved about 2 more marks than pupils at schools in the Inner Harbour region, with pupils in the South Eastern region achieving the highest marks.

As a follow-up to the findings on region, it could be noted that the region variable was not really relevant to church and independent schools, since they typically draw their pupils from a wide catchment area. For this reason, the analyses were repeated, confining attention to those in state schools only. The results are shown in the last panel of Table 6.1. From this further analysis, it was clear that state schools in the Inner Harbour were on average indeed lagging behind, and it was only the performance of pupils in private schools that disguised this.

6.2 English

Table 6.2 shows the results of multilevel analyses, first with all the variables taken singly ('unadjusted'), and then including all variables simultaneously ('adjusted').

Pupil Variables

6.2.1 Gender

The column labelled *N* gives the numbers of girls and boys. The unadjusted difference in attainment between girls and boys was 0.76, much larger than the standard error of this difference (0.20). This suggests that the difference was statistically significant. Girls performed better than boys, by around three quarters of a mark on average. This can be compared with a population standard deviation of 15 marks.

6.2.2 Age

Older pupils performed significantly better than younger pupils as for the Maltese test. The coefficient was 0.14, which means that for every month older a pupil will score 0.14 marks more.

6.2.3 Language

Pupils who spoke English as a first language performed better than pupils whose first language was Maltese. The difference in marks was about 2.5 when pupils' language was considered alone. However this difference dropped to just over 1 mark when all other variables were also accounted for. This indicated that other factors contributed to this difference.

Table 6.2: Unadjusted and Adjusted Results: English

			Unadjusted model			Adjusted model		
		N	Coefficient	s.e.	Chi-square	Coefficient	s.e.	Chi-square
Pupil variables								
Gender	Boys	2542	0	–	15.0***	0	–	12.0***
	Girls	2431	0.76	0.196		0.61	0.177	
Age	In years and (completed) months	4973	0.14	0.025	29.6***	0.12	0.023	26.9***
First language	Maltese	4586	0	–	34.1***	0	–	11.5***
	English	357	2.49	0.427		1.12	0.394	
	Other (inc. bilingual)	30	-0.66	1.168		-1.79	1.065	
SEN	None	4752	0	–	345.0***	0	–	280.8***
	Mild to moderate	157	-8.06	0.522		-6.95	0.496	
	Severe to very severe	64	-9.26	0.803		-7.83	0.757	
Home variables								
Mother's Education	Other	191	0	–	350.0***	0	–	67.7***
	No formal schooling	15	-0.97	1.644		-0.47	1.745	
	Primary School	414	-0.65	0.594		-0.89	0.657	
	Secondary School	3470	2.87	0.511		1.14	0.582	
	Pre-university courses and vocational courses	504	5.43	0.569		2.20	0.639	
	Tertiary Education	379	6.61	0.588		3.09	0.681	

Father's Education	Other	286	0	–	334.9***	0	–	25.2***
	No formal schooling	22	-0.31	1.354		-0.84	1.446	
	Primary School	511	0.67	0.482		0.32	0.577	
	Secondary School	2978	2.96	0.407		0.83	0.519	
	Pre-university courses and vocational courses	507	5.23	0.480		1.77	0.585	
	Tertiary Education	669	6.38	0.460		2.02	0.594	
Mother's Occupation	Other	3694	0	–	155.8***	0	–	24.6***
	Professional	261	3.42	0.405		0.57	0.444	
	Managerial and administrative	164	2.41	0.510		0.44	0.488	
	Higher clerical, skilled craftsmen, technicians	372	2.92	0.342		1.38	0.330	
	Skilled manual workers and foremen	160	1.06	0.502		0.83	0.466	
	Semi-skilled, unskilled workers, labourers	322	-1.04	0.370		-0.62	0.343	
Father's Occupation	Other	443	0	–	386.6***	0	–	99.1***
	Professional	411	6.53	0.437		2.96	0.512	
	Managerial and administrative	837	5.40	0.376		2.89	0.410	
	Higher clerical, skilled craftsmen, technicians	848	4.30	0.365		2.27	0.393	
	Skilled manual workers and foremen	1471	2.20	0.336		0.92	0.362	
	Semi-skilled, unskilled workers, labourers	963	1.17	0.353		0.29	0.375	

Table 6.2: Unadjusted and Adjusted Results: English (continued)

			Unadjusted model			Adjusted model		
		N	Coefficient	s.e.	Chi-square	Coefficient	s.e.	Chi-square
School variables								
No. Year 5 classes	1	531	0	–	3.8	0	–	11.3
	2	1301	-1.09	0.975		-0.48	0.503	
	3	1034	-0.88	1.172		-0.78	0.587	
	4	811	-0.75	1.319		-1.34	0.735	
	5	808	-2.55	1.473		-2.86	0.961	
	6	124	-2.55	3.663		-1.79	1.777	
	7	166	-2.51	3.652		0.27	1.764	
	9	198	-2.36	3.647		-3.13	1.909	
Type of School	Primary B State School	1588	0	–	96.9***	0	–	76.5***
	Primary C State School	1529	-0.35	0.624		-1.43	0.783	
	Private Independent School	598	7.59	0.828		4.10	0.826	
	Private Church School	1258	4.75	0.682		2.54	0.829	
Region	Inner Harbour	1290	0	–	3.3	0	–	13.0**
	Outer Harbour	1437	1.40	1.043		1.81	0.568	
	South Eastern	612	-0.71	1.262		1.52	0.656	
	Western	672	0.75	1.257		1.06	0.618	
	Northern	572	1.02	1.460		1.99	0.800	
	Gozo	390	0.61	1.194		1.24	0.620	
State schools only								
Region	Inner Harbour	411	0	–	27.4***	0	–	15.6**
	Outer Harbour	966	3.38	0.79		2.44	0.78	
	South Eastern	564	3.44	0.84		2.04	0.75	
	Western	473	3.52	0.90		2.04	0.79	
	Northern	417	3.84	0.98		2.73	0.93	
	Gozo	286	4.53	0.89		2.58	0.77	

6.2.4 Special Educational Needs

As with the Maltese test, the largest impact on pupils' raw score was their level of special educational needs. Pupils with mild to moderate levels of Special Educational Needs scored about 8 points lower than pupils without any SEN and 7 points lower after adjusting for other factors. Pupils with severe to very severe levels of SEN obtained raw scores about 9 points lower and 8 points lower after taking other factors into consideration. Many, though not all, pupils who were classified as having Special Educational Needs had learning difficulties.

Home Variables

6.2.5 Mother's Education

Pupils whose mothers were educated to secondary school level or higher, achieved higher raw scores. Pupils whose mothers had tertiary education, obtained raw scores over 7 marks higher than pupils whose mothers had no formal education, when this was the only variable in the model. This difference dropped to 3 marks when other variables were also accounted for.

6.2.6 Father's Education

As with the Maltese test, the same relationship existed with the father's level of education. However pupils whose fathers were educated to primary school level or above achieved higher raw scores than their peers.

6.2.7 Parental Occupation

The mothers' occupation had a significant impact on their children's scores. Pupils whose mothers were categorised as 'professional' or 'higher clerical, skilled craftsmen, technicians' gained around 3 marks more on average than the majority of pupils whose mothers were in the 'other' category (mainly homemakers), while pupils whose mothers were in the 'semi-skilled, unskilled workers, labourers' group obtained about 1 mark less on average. This pattern was less strong when other variables were also taken into account.

The **fathers' occupation** significantly impacted on their children's raw score and followed the ordering of the classification itself, though again these effects became smaller after allowing for other factors.

The **mother's occupation** appeared to have a smaller effect than the father's. This was not surprising because most mothers fell into the group labelled 'Other' (presumably homemakers) which was used as a baseline. The mothers' occupation seemed to have the lowest effect of the parental education and occupation groupings, both before and after taking the other factors into account. However, this effect was still substantial.

School Variables

6.2.8 Number of Year 5 Classes

Some differences in raw scores were detected depending on the number of Year 5 classes in the school. Usually pupils in schools with 1 class gained a point or two more than pupils in schools with more than 1 class. However these differences were not statistically significant.

6.2.9 Type of School

Pupils attending independent and church schools performed better than those who attended state schools, by about 5 or 8 marks. Differences dropped significantly after taking other factors into account, although they remained statistically significant.

6.2.10 Region

In the 'unadjusted' model (considering each variable in exclusion of any other) pupils performed at the same level irrespective of the region of Malta that their school was situated in. However, when all other variables were accounted for, pupils performed differentially across the regions. Pupils from most regions gained at least one extra mark, on average, compared to those from the Inner Harbour, while pupils from the Northern region gained around 2 more marks. This was quite a surprising result, since it was generally observed that adjusting for such social factors would reduce, rather than increase, existing differences.

As a follow-up to the findings on region, it could be noted that the region variable was not really relevant to church and independent schools, since they typically draw their pupils from a wide catchment area. For this reason, the analyses were repeated, confining attention to those in state schools only. The results are shown in the last panel of Table 6.2. From this further analysis, it became clear that state schools in the Inner Harbour region were on average indeed lagging behind, and it was only the performance of pupils in private schools that disguised this. Even after adjusting for other factors, pupils in state schools in other areas achieved at least 2 marks more than pupils in state schools in the Inner Harbour region.

6.3 Summary of the Multilevel Modelling Results for the Maltese Test

Pupil Variables

- Girls performed better than boys, by around one mark on average.
- Older pupils performed significantly better than younger pupils by about 0.15 marks for every month older.
- Pupils who did not speak Maltese as their first language performed less well than those who did. Pupils who spoke other languages (which includes bilingual children) achieved about 3 marks fewer than native Maltese speaking pupils. Pupils who spoke English as their first language obtained, on average, just over 1 mark lower than their Maltese speaking peers. However this dropped to about 3

marks when all other variables were taken into account.

- Special Educational Needs on average had the most effect on pupils' raw score. Pupils with mild to moderate levels of Special Educational Needs scored about 7 or 8 points lower than pupils without any SEN. Pupils with severe to very severe levels of SEN obtained raw scores of about 9 or 10 points lower. Many, though not all, pupils who were classified as having Special Educational Needs had learning difficulties.

Home Variables

- Pupils whose mothers were educated to at least secondary school level achieved higher raw scores than pupils whose mothers had lower levels of education. Their average raw scores ranged from 4 to 6 marks more and rose with the level of their mother's education. This difference in marks dropped to 1 or 2 marks when all other variables were taken into account.
- The same relationship existed with fathers' level of education.
- Fathers' current occupation significantly impacted on their children's raw score and followed the ordering of the classification itself.
- Not many categories of mothers' occupations were indicated as being significantly related to their children's raw score, whereas most of the fathers' occupational categories were. This is not unsurprising because most mothers fell into the group labelled 'Other' (presumably homemakers) which was used as a baseline. However, even fewer categories were significant in the adjusted model. This implies that little could be attributed to mothers' occupations once their levels of education had been taken into account. Mothers' occupation seemed to have the lowest effect of the parental education and occupation

groupings both before and after taking the other factors into account: however this effect was still substantial.

School Variables

- Some differences in raw scores were detected depending on the number of Year 5 classes in the school. However there was no obvious pattern to the differential performance.
- Pupils attending private and church schools performed better than those who attend state schools, by about 2 or 3 marks.
- Pupils in different regions of Malta performed differentially. Pupils from most regions achieved about 2 more marks than pupils at schools in the Inner Harbour region, with pupils in the South Eastern region achieving the highest marks.

6.4 Summary of the Multilevel Modelling Results for the English Test

Pupil Variables

- Girls performed better than boys, by less than one mark on average.
- Older pupils performed significantly better than younger pupils by about 0.14 marks more for every month older.
- Pupils who spoke English as their first language performed better than pupils whose first language was Maltese. The difference in marks was about 2.5 when pupils' language was considered alone. However this difference dropped to just over 1 mark when all other variables were also accounted for. This indicates that other factors contributed to this.
- As with the Maltese test, the largest impact on pupils' raw score was their level of Special Educational Need. Pupils

with some degree of Special Educational Need scored about 8 points less than their peers.

Home Variables

- Pupils whose mothers were educated to secondary school level or higher achieved higher raw scores. Pupils whose mothers had tertiary education obtained raw scores of 6 marks higher than pupils whose mothers had no formal education, when this was the only variable in the model. This difference dropped to just less than 3 marks when other variables were also accounted for.
- As with the Maltese test, the same relationship existed with fathers' level of education. The same relationship between fathers' occupation and their children's raw scores existed as in the Maltese test, that is, it followed the ordering of the classification itself.
- Unlike the Maltese test, mothers' occupation had a significant impact on their children's scores. Pupils whose mothers were categorised as 'professional' or 'higher clerical, skilled craftsmen, technicians' gained around 3 marks more on average than the majority of pupils whose mothers were in the 'other' category. While pupils whose mothers were in the 'semi-skilled, unskilled workers, labourers' group obtained about 1 mark less on average. This pattern was less strong when other variables were also taken into account.

School Variables

- The number of Year 5 classes in the school did not affect pupils' raw scores.
- As with the Maltese test, pupils attending private and church schools performed better than those attending state schools.
- In the 'unadjusted' model (considering each variable in

exclusion of any other) pupils performed at the same level irrespective of the region of Malta that their school was situated in. Whereas, when all other variables were accounted for, pupils performed differentially across the regions. Pupils from most regions gained at least one extra mark, on average, compared to those from the Inner Harbour, while pupils from the Northern region gained around 2 more marks. This is quite a surprising result, since it is generally observed that adjusting for such social factors reduces, rather than increases, existing differences.

Chapter 7

Implications and Recommendations

7.1 Implications

The March 2002 Year 5 Literacy study is the second major study of the literacy situation in primary schools in Malta to have been conducted by the Literacy Unit of Malta, and like the earlier study (Mifsud et al., 2000) it has proved a considerable success, with a remarkable response rate. It is also worth noting that, as with the earlier study, it proved necessary to produce from scratch a completely new test for Maltese. We believe that this test, along with that produced for the Year 2 Literacy Study, will be of value to Maltese schools in the years to come.

These analyses have looked at the overall performance of Maltese Year 5 pupils in literacy for Maltese and English, as well as comparing the performance of groups defined by a number of factors. Not only has the performance of these groups been compared, but we have also considered, using the technique of multilevel modelling, whether these factors have an effect on their own, or whether they might be caused, in their turn, by other factors.

The analysis of the National Literacy Survey 2002 showed that, like the results from the previous survey, girls still perform better than boys and that independent and church schools do better than state schools even more so for English than for Maltese. The results also showed that pupils in schools in the Inner Harbour area do worse at literacy than do pupils in virtually any other area. Worryingly, these regional differences become worse, rather than better, when allowance is made for the home background of the pupils.

7.2 Recommendations

- The main recommendations from the first Malta National Literacy Survey (2000) were that not only the survey be repeated in a number of years' time but also that action be taken to ensure boys do not fall behind in the important life skill of literacy and that children achieving a relatively low raw score in either language be identified to schools, so that intensive individual support can be given to any of these children not already receiving it.
- Results from these analyses show that boys are still performing lower than girls and also that some pupils obtain relatively low raw scores on the tests.
- In order to investigate if initiatives to improve the performance of some groups of pupils are effective it is necessary to utilise both sets of test results. Analysing pupils' Year 2 test results matched to their Year 5 test results allows us to consider how much 'progress' either individual or groups of pupils are making between the successive rounds of testing.
- Therefore following the two National Literacy Surveys (1999, 2002), the next step was to conduct a value added study of education in Maltese primary schools over the three-year period from Year 2 to Year 5. The data from the two studies was successfully merged. The results of this analysis are reported in Section Two of this publication.

7.3 Making International Comparisons

The Malta Year 5 Literacy Study uses two tests, one of Maltese, and one of English. The Maltese test was devised specifically for this study, and has been used on this single occasion so far. Though we believe that it will be of value in the future, either for surveys of trends in Maltese reading attainment over time, or for the assessment of individual pupils, it provides no basis for comparison with other occasions or locations.

The situation is different for the English test, which is a standard instrument, namely the *Reading Progress Test 3* in the Hodder and Stoughton Assessing Reading 7-11 series (Vincent et al., 1997). The manual for this test gives norms and age equivalents for England and Wales, thus offering the opportunity for comparison with the UK.

There is a complication that some pupils did the Maltese test first, and some did the English test first. The recommended procedure was that alternate pupils should take English and Maltese first, but in some schools all pupils took the same test first. To avoid the possibility of a carry-over from one test to another, we confined the analysis to pupils who had taken the English test first. In fact, there was a tendency for private schools to take the English test first, and for state schools to take the Maltese test first, perhaps because they felt that it would be easier for the pupils to encounter the more familiar language first. The results were reweighted to allow for this.

The Reading Progress Test (RPT) manual states that the test was standardised on a national sample of 2014 children from 139 schools in 17 local authorities in England and Wales, though no further details are given. The results quoted in the RPT manual for age equivalents give an age equivalent of 108 months for a score of 22, compared with the figures from the Year 5 National Literacy Survey of 116 and 22 to the nearest whole number.

From this one may conclude that despite the fact that most Maltese children learn English as a second language, rather than as native speakers, on the average they are within about 8 months of native speakers in the UK.

Table 7.1: Mean Test Scores for Malta

	Mean score	N	Mean Age
Reweighted sample score	22.4	2348	115.7

Comparisons are also possible for Year 2. The test used was the *Reading Progress Baseline*. We reweighted the results in a comparable way as for the Year 5 scores. The mean score in Malta was 29.8 and the mean age was 80 months. The results quoted in the England and Wales RPT manual for age equivalents give an age equivalent of 74 months for this score, i.e. some 6 months behind.

It seems that the Maltese pupils have largely managed to 'keep up' with the native speakers in England and Wales, making essentially comparable progress over the three years, despite only learning English as a second language.

Annex I

School Questionnaire

(TO BE COMPLETED BY THE HEAD OR THE ASSISTANT HEAD)
It would be very helpful if you could provide the following background information on your school. Please circle or mark one answer for each item. Thank you.

1. Type of school:
   Primary B State School 1
   Primary C State School 2
   Private Independent School 3
   Private Church School.. 4

2. Geographical region of the school:
   (Please refer to the attached classification)

   Inner Harbour 1
   Outer Harbour 2
   South Eastern 3
   Western.. 4
   Northern 5
   Gozo 6

3. Number of pupils in **Year 5** in 2001/2:

   _______ boys (1)
   _______ girls (2)

THANK YOU VERY MUCH FOR COMPLETING THIS QUESTIONNAIRE.

Annex II

Geographical Regions

The classification of the Geographical Regions of the Maltese Islands as used by the National Statistics Office is as follows:

1. Inner Harbour
Valletta, Floriana, Marsa, Senglea, Cospicua, Vittoriosa, Kalkara, Paola, Sliema, Gzira, Msida, Hamrun, Pietà.

2. Outer Harbour
Zabbar, Xghajra, Fgura, Tarxien, Luqa, Qormi, Birkirkara, Santa Venera, St.Julian's, San Gwann, Santa Lucia, Pembroke.

3. South Eastern
Marsascala, Gudja, Ghaxaq, Zejtun, Marsaxlokk, Birzebbugia, Mqabba, Kirkop, Safi, Qrendi, Zurrieq.

4. Western
Zebbug, Siggiewi, Dingli, Lija, Attard, Mtarfa, Rabat, Bahrija.

5. Northern
Naxxar, Gharghur, Mellieha, St. Paul's Bay, Mosta, Mgarr.

6. Gozo
Gharb, Zebbug, Xaghra, Kercem, Victoria, Nadur, Qala, Sannat, Xewkija, Ghajnsielem, San Lawrenz.

Annex III

Classification of Occupations

The classification of the occupations of parents of pupils who participated in this study is based on Vassallo et al. (1994) but is adapted to suit the needs of this study, and is as follows:

1. Professional
(Medical doctor, teacher, lecturer, engineer, architect, lawyer)

2. Managerial & Administrative
(Manager, sergeant, director, Administrative officer)

3. Higher clerical, skilled craftsmen, technicians
(Policeman, mail officer, decorator, secretary, dental hygienist, electrician, miller, carpenter, surveyor, supervisor, draughtsman)

4. Skilled manual workers, foremen
(Plumber, stone mason, builder, fisherman, driver, fitter, security guard, soldier, vegetable seller, hairdresser, confectioner, mechanic)

5. Semi-skilled or unskilled workers, labourers
(Plasterer, factory worker, waiter, white-washer, cleaner, pump attendant messenger)

6. Income provided by the state
(Receiving state benefits, pension)

7. Not known

8. Deceased

Annex IV

Pupil Data Form

National Survey Of Literacy Attainment Of Year 5 Pupils (2002)

School Name:______________________________

School Code:_________________

1 Pupil No.	2 Surname	3 Name	4 Date of birth d/m/y	5 Gender Male: 1 Female: 2	6 First Lang.	7 Father's Occup.	8 Mother's Occup.	9 Father's Educ.	10 Mother's Educ.	11 S.E.N.	12 Pre-school Educ.	13 Absentees Eng.	14 Mlt.

Literacy Unit 2002

Annex V

Test Administrators' Questionnaire

Suitability and Manageability Questions:

1. In your opinion, how suitable was the Maltese language test for the pupils in your school who took it?
Very suitable Fairly suitable Borderline Unsuitable

2. In your opinion, how suitable was the English language test for the pupils in your school who took it?
Very suitable Fairly suitable Borderline Unsuitable

3. In your opinion, how manageable was the Maltese language test to administer in your school?
Very manageable Fairly manageable Borderline Unmanageable

4. In your opinion, how manageable was the English language test to administer in your school?
Very manageable Fairly manageable Borderline Unmanageable

5. Please write any comments about the tests.

English test:

____

____

____

Maltese test:

____

____

____

THANK YOU VERY MUCH FOR COMPLETING THIS QUESTIONNAIRE.

Section Two

A National Value Added Study of Year 2 to Year 5 Pupils

Introduction

Differences between observed average results for schools may be due partly to differences in the knowledge pupils came equipped with from home or previous schooling at kindergarten level, on entering primary school, and partly due to differences in the progress made by the pupils during their time at the school.

The questions which we tackled in this Value Added Study included:

- Were there significant differences in the progress made by pupils in different types of schools between Year 2 and Year 5?
- What factors were related to differences in pupil progress from Year 2 to Year 5?
- Did pupils in different types of schools, or in schools in different parts of the country, make more progress?

Chapter 8

Methodological Issues

8.1 Data Collection

The National Literacy Study of Year 2 pupils (1999) collected information on pupils' performance in reading in both Maltese and English. The same pupils were tested again in Year 5, that is, three years later in 2002. The research involved statistical analysis of a specially-constructed national value added dataset from Year 2 to Year 5, which matched the records for pupils in Year 5 back to the records for the corresponding pupils in Year 2. Among those schools for which identifiable data were available on both occasions, the National Foundation for Educational Research in England and Wales (NFER), with the co-operation of the University of Malta and the schools themselves, was able to match some 97 per cent of pupils.

The vast majority of pupils were matched on school, first name, surname and date of birth. This matching was carried out using a combination of computer matching and visual inspection. Following this step the schools checked matches, and further matching was carried out using the information thus obtained. This figure of 97 per cent was impressively high, and compared very favourably with those for comparable exercises in the UK.

8.2 The Matching Process

Initial data was provided in two files, one containing 5420 records for pupils in Year 2 and one containing 5466 records for the same cohort in Year 5.

A series of matching runs was carried out, using school ID, forename, surname and date of birth to match records. Four main matching runs were undertaken. At each stage successful matches were removed and the remaining records checked by eye before moving to the next run. The runs followed a descending order of match security. First pupils were matched on four fields: first name, surname, date of birth and school. The remaining pupils were scanned by eye, and obvious amendments to dates and the spelling of names were made. In many cases the Year 2 dates were simply the Year 5 dates but recorded under the US, rather than the UK convention, and in these cases the Year 2 dates were amended to consistency. In other cases pupils' names appeared to have been recorded using slightly different orthographic conventions.

The school ID variable was not used from this point on when matching the remaining records. Pupils were then matched on forename, surname and date of birth. Finally pupils were matched on forename and surname only after any name amendments had been made. This category was checked with particular care, as it offered the widest scope for mismatches. It should be noted that numbers here were relatively small and there was little, if any, scope for confusion. Once it was not possible to have further matches, the entire matching syntax was run as a single process to produce the final data file.

Over 5000 records were examined by eye during the matching exercise, as each stage of the process revealed more corrections to be made. By the end of the exercise, approximately 15% of the Year 2 forename data and 5% of the surname data had been amended. Most of the amendments were due to simple typographical errors, but middle names, double-barrelled names, abbreviations, various forms of apostrophe and different orthographic conventions also caused problems.

After this preliminary matching exercise, pupil lists were returned to the participating schools to enable them to check for accuracy and matching. Three lists were sent to schools, matched cases, unmatched Year 2 cases and unmatched Year 5 cases. At this stage schools also helped in the matching

Table 8.1: Process of Matching Year 2 to Year 5 Dataset

Matching on	Frequency	Percent	Cumulative Percent
Forename, surname only	67	1.2	1.2
Forename, surname, date of birth	86	1.5	2.7
Forename, surname, reversed format date of birth	1	0.0	2.7
School, forename, surname	1258	22.2	25.0
School, forename, surname, date of birth	3465	61.3	86.2
School, forename, surname, reversed format date of birth	90	1.6	87.8
Former school, forename, surname	122	2.2	90.0
Former school, forename, surname, date of birth	134	2.4	92.4
Former school, forename, surname, reversed format date of birth	8	0.1	92.5
Total cases matched	5231	92.5	
Information provided by Malta did not lead to a match	59	1.0	93.5
Child has moved to a school for which Y5 data not supplied	1	0.0	93.6
Child moved to a Special school/unit	3	0.1	93.6
Y2 unmatched- no information provided by Malta	29	0.5	94.1
Child held back 1 year or advanced 1 year	170	3.0	97.1
Deceased	1	0.0	97.2
Y5 unmatched- no information provided by Malta	46	0.8	98.0
Child absent for either test	10	0.2	98.1
Malta expressed inability to provide further information	27	0.5	98.6
Y2 unmatchable- child has left Malta	32	0.6	99.2
Y5 unmatchable- last school abroad	46	0.8	100.0
Total	5655	100	

process by indicating either the destination or origin of unmatched pupils. For example some pupils had left the country, while others had changed their surname and gone to a different school. After incorporating this information from schools, it proved possible to match 92.5 per cent of all the original cases.

Not all of the children were matchable. As indicated above, some had emigrated, while others attended a school which had not supplied Year 2 information or which had supplied information in an anonymous form, thus preventing matching. After excluding such 'impossible' cases, 97.2 % of cases were matched. Probably the bulk of remaining unmatched cases result from children being known by forename or middle name at different periods of time.

The final file contained 5655 records. Of these, 5231 were eventually matched. Matched and unmatched data were broken down as seen in Table 8.1.

8.3 The Sample

A total of 5231 pupils were matched from the Year 2 and the Year 5 datasets. Pupils with out of range or missing data were excluded from the value added analysis. These criteria included only those born in 1992, and we also removed pupils who did not have a full complement of Year 2 and Year 5 results in the English and Maltese tests. Having made these selections the sample used for this value added study contained 4,239 pupils from 96 schools in Malta. (Three schools could not be included because they did not provide identifiable data). The sample can be described in terms of the school-level, pupil-level and the home background variables that were collected. Table 8.2 on opposite page shows the school types and regions of the schools attended by these pupils.

In terms of the pupil-level factors, there were slightly more girls than boys in the value added study; 50.3% and 49.7% respectively

Table 8.2: Table of School Variables

	No. of Pupils	Percentage of Pupils	No. of schools
Type of school			
Primary A/B State schools	1466	34.6	17
Primary C State schools	1306	30.8	45
Private Independent schools	365	8.6	9
Private Church schools	1102	26.0	25
Region			
Inner Harbour	1090	25.7	30
Outer Harbour	1214	28.6	20
South Eastern	576	13.6	12
Western	597	14.1	12
Northern	388	10.2	7
Gozo	318	7.8	15
Total	4239	100	96

(2131 girls and 2108 boys). The great majority (93.8%) of these pupils spoke Maltese as their first language. A number of pupils had some level of special educational needs (SEN); 2.8% at a mild to moderate level and 1.2% at a severe or very severe level. The SEN level of 12.5% of the pupils had changed since Year 2. Schools were allowed discretion in deciding whether to enter pupils for the test, if it was likely to cause them distress. As the Year 5 test was more difficult than the Year 2 one, it was more likely to upset pupils of modest ability, and it seems that fewer special needs pupils were entered in the test in Year 5 than in Year 2 (4 per cent, as opposed to 12 per cent). There were also some small differences in the way that this information was recorded in the data collected.

As well as school-level and pupil-level factors, some home variables were also collected. Both the mother's and father's highest level of education and their current occupations were recorded. These are detailed in Table 8.3.

Table 8.3: Table of Home Variables

	Percentage of Fathers	Percentage of Mothers
Occupation		
Professional	7	5
Managerial & administrative	16	3
Higher clerical, skilled craftsmen, technicians	18	7
Skilled manual workers, foremen	31	3
Semi/un-skilled workers, labourers	20	7
Other	8	75
Education		
No formal schooling	0.4	0.3
Primary School	10	8
Secondary School	62	72
Pre-university courses and vocational courses	10	9
University Education	13	7
Other	5	3
Total	4239	4239

8.4 Age-standardised Scores

An age–standardisation on a British sample already existed for the *Reading Progress Test* series (Vincent et al., 1996). For a discussion of how the age-standardisation procedure was conducted see Section 1.5, pages 21 and 22.

Chapter 9

Modelling Carried Out

9.1 Multilevel Modelling

The main analysis was carried out on the full dataset linking Year 2 test scores in Maltese and English in 1999 to Year 5 results in both languages in 2002. This contained matched data on 5231 pupils in 99 schools.

From this data we carried out linear multilevel modelling of comparative progress in literacy in:

- Maltese, allowing for the pupils' attainment in Year 2.
- Maltese, allowing for the pupils' attainment in Year 2 and their home background.
- English, allowing for the pupils' attainment in Year 2.
- English, allowing for the pupils' attainment in Year 2 and their home background.

Chapter 10 contains details of these modelling exercises.

The modelling was carried out on a slightly smaller dataset linking scores on literacy in Maltese and English in Year 2 in 1999 to scores on literacy in Maltese and English in Year 5 in 2002 for the same pupils. This analysis contained data for 4199 pupils in 96 of the 99 schools in Malta. For technical reasons it was not possible to link Year 2 and Year 5 data for pupils at the remaining schools. In addition to literacy data, it proved possible to include a substantial amount of detail on pupils' home background in the analyses.

9.2 Variables Used for Multilevel Modelling

In Section One, the relationships between various factors on pupils' performance in Year 5 in tests of literacy in Maltese and English were explored. Here the dataset is enriched by the

Table 9.1: Variables Collected for Multilevel Modelling

Pupil variables	
Prior Attainment	Standardised scores obtained in Year 2
Gender	Boy
	Girl
Age	In Years and (completed) Months
First Language	Maltese
	Not Maltese
Special Educational Needs	None
	Mild to moderate
	Severe to very severe
	Change in level of special educational needs
Home variables	
Mother's Education	No formal schooling
	Primary school
	Secondary school
	Pre-university courses and vocational courses
	University education
	Other
	Increase in educational level since Year 2
Father's Education	No formal schooling
	Primary school
	Secondary school
	Pre-university courses and vocational courses
	University education
	Other
Mother's Occupation	Professional
	Managerial and administrative
	Higher clerical, skilled craftsmen, technicians
	Skilled manual workers, foremen
	Semi-skilled, unskilled workers, labourers
	Other
Father's Occupation	Professional
	Managerial and administrative
	Higher clerical, skilled craftsmen, technicians
	Skilled manual workers, foremen
	Semi-skilled, unskilled workers, labourers
	Other
School variables	
Number of Year 5 Classes in the School	1 - 7, 9
Number of Year 2 Classes in the School	1 – 8

Type of School	Primary A/B state school
	Primary C state school
	Private independent School
	Private church school
Region of the School	Inner Harbour
	Outer Harbour
	South Eastern
	Western
	Northern
	Gozo

incorporation of test scores at two time points. This allows us to examine progress between Years 2 and 5.

The data was modelled on two levels: pupils and schools. Variables that were used in the models are detailed in Table 9.1.

The modelling also investigated 'change variables', that is, variables which depicted change in status since Year 2 (for example, change in level of special educational needs). Some of these were originally included in the modelling process but were removed because they did not turn out to be statistically significant. Results are presented in Table 9.1 only for the change variables that were significant.

Two different multilevel models were employed. In the first model the prior attainment measure was included, allowing us to evaluate progress rather than performance. Each of the variables was included in the model individually on top of prior attainment. This allowed us to determine the impact of each of the factors separately. This model is referred to as being *'adjusted for prior attainment'*. The second model included all the variables together so that each variable is considered simultaneously with all the other factors that may affect pupil's progress. This is referred to as the *'fully adjusted'* model.

The results arising from the use of these models are given in Chapter 10. Detailed results (tabulations of the coefficients, standard errors and tests of significance) for both the models; adjusted for prior attainment only and fully adjusted, are provided after the summary results in the following chapter.

Chapter 10

Results of the Multilevel Analysis

In this section, the results of the multilevel analyses are described first for Maltese and then for English.

10.1 Maltese

Table 10.1 shows the results of the multilevel analyses for the Maltese test, first with all the variables taken singly but adjusted only for prior attainment ('adjusted for pretest'), and then including all variables simultaneously ('adjusted'). The aim of this sort of analysis is to estimate the differences between the subgroups when as many of the other potential influences as possible are taken into account.

In the description that follows, there is reference to 'standardised score points' at various points in describing the size of an effect. The size of these 'standardised score points' may be interpreted by noting that 15 standardised score points is equivalent to one population standard deviation. Two thirds of the population lie within one standard deviation of the mean. Only differences that were statistically significant at the .05 level are reported below.

Pupil Variables

10.1.1 Gender

Allowing for their performance in Year 2, girls and boys had made the same amount of progress by Year 5. Girls were already ahead in Year 2, so this meant that the differential was maintained.

10.1.2 Age

Older and younger pupils made equivalent progress.

Table 10.1: Multilevel Modelling Results for the Maltese Test

			Unadjusted for pretest			Fully adjusted model		
		N	Coefficient	s.e.	Chi-square	Coefficient	s.e.	Chi-square
Pupil variables								
Prior Attainment in Maltese	Standardised Score in Year 2	4239	0.61	0.01	1859.0***	0.51	0.01	1197.6***
Sex	Boys	2108	0	–	0.7	0	–	0.2
	Girls	2131	0.31	0.37		0.15	0.36	
Age	In years and (completed) months	4239	-0.03	0.05	0.5	-0.06	0.05	1.6
First Language	Maltese	3866	0	–	0.3	0	–	9.8**
	Not Maltese	373	-0.41	0.75		-2.35	0.75	
SEN	None	4072	0	–	148.0***	0	–	134.9***
	Mild to moderate	118	-9.22	1.12		-8.79	1.12	
	Severe to very severe	49	-11.77	1.76		-10.81	1.74	
	Change in level of SEN since Year 2	530	5.59	0.57		5.35	0.56	
Home variables								
Mother's Education	Other	134	0	–	83.4***	0	–	15.2*
	No formal schooling	12	1.30	3.35		-2.89	3.56	
	Primary School	355	2.64	1.21		0.40	1.38	
	Secondary School	3049	4.43	1.06		0.78	1.24	
	Pre-university courses and vocational courses	391	8.27	1.21		3.14	1.40	
	University Education	298	8.25	1.27		2.71	1.49	
	Increase in mother's education since Year 2	685	-1.34	0.55		-0.74	0.54	

Table 10.1: Multilevel Modelling Results for the Maltese Test (continued)

			Unadjusted for pretest			Fully adjusted model		
		N	Coefficient	s.e.	Chi-square	Coefficient	s.e.	Chi-square
Father's Education	Other	209	0	–	121.7***	0	–	23.8***
	No formal schooling	16	7.20	2.86		7.70	3.07	
	Primary School	444	3.85	0.96		2.93	1.20	
	Secondary School	2629	5.41	0.83		3.92	1.09	
	Pre-university courses and vocational courses	406	8.00	0.98		4.99	1.22	
	University Education	535	9.17	0.94		5.40	1.25	
Mother's Occupation	Other	3188	0	–	37.7***	0	–	9.9
	Professional	210	2.91	0.81		0.52	0.92	
	Managerial and administrative	114	1.83	1.08		-0.15	1.08	
	Higher clerical, skilled craftsmen, technicians	310	2.44	0.67		1.07	0.68	
	Skilled manual workers and foremen	140	1.02	0.96		1.11	0.93	
	Semi-skilled, unskilled workers, labourers	277	-2.12	0.71		-1.59	0.70	
Father's Occupation	Other	357	0	–	117.2***	0	–	29.6***
	Professional	314	7.60	0.90		3.14	1.09	
	Managerial and administrative	664	5.94	0.76		2.70	0.86	
	Higher clerical, skilled craftsmen, technicians	750	4.60	0.73		1.58	0.81	
	Skilled manual workers and foremen	1306	2.42	0.67		0.01	0.76	
	Semi-skilled, unskilled workers, labourers	848	1.84	0.70		-0.17	0.78	

School variables								
No. of Year 5 Classes	1	439	0	–	4.0	0	–	5.3
	2	1157	-0.57	1.21		0.23	1.34	
	3	889	-1.38	1.41		-0.81	1.61	
	4	577	-0.69	1.68		0.51	1.95	
	5	725	-3.02	1.73		-3.68	2.09	
	6	118	-1.42	4.15		-3.78	4.15	
	7	155	-2.23	4.12		-1.74	4.82	
	9	179	1.91	4.10		0.94	4.12	
No. of Year 2 Classes	1	495	0	–	2.3	0	–	1.5
	2	1234	-1.06	0.98		-0.84	1.11	
	3	879	-1.67	1.12		-1.09	1.33	
	4	714	-0.85	1.23		-0.78	1.47	
	5	433	-1.31	1.48		-0.31	1.70	
	6	248	-0.88	1.80		0.18	1.97	
	7	151	-1.01	2.71		1.13	3.32	
	8	85	-0.83	1.91		-0.92	2.07	
Type of School	State School	2772	0	–	3.1	0	–	0.1
	Private School	1467	1.66	0.94		0.19	0.94	
Region	Inner Harbour	1090	0	–	4.0	0	–	7.1
	Outer Harbour	1214	1.88	1.25		3.21	1.25	
	South Eastern	576	0.85	1.50		2.50	1.47	
	Western	597	1.08	1.48		1.20	1.34	
	Northern	431	1.86	1.81		1.63	1.81	
	Gozo	331	2.49	1.46		1.98	1.39	

10.1.3 First Language

When accounting for their performance in Year 2, pupils whose first language was not Maltese made equivalent progress to their peers. However, adjusting for all other variables as well as Year 2 performance, pupils whose first language is not Maltese made less progress, by just over 2 standardised score points.

10.1.4 Special Educational Needs

Pupils' level of Special Educational Needs (SEN) had a very significant relationship with their progress in both the model adjusted for prior attainment only and the fully adjusted model. When accounting for no factors other than pupils' prior attainment and level of SEN, pupils with mild to moderate SEN made around 9 standardised score points less progress than pupils with no SEN, while pupils with severe to very severe SEN made about 12 standardised score points less progress. When accounting for all other factors these differences in progress had decreased to around 9 and 11 standardised score points respectively. A change in pupil's level of SEN from Year 2 to Year 5 resulted in a change in their progress. This change was an increase or decrease of about 5 standardised score points as their SEN level decreased or increased, respectively. The precise size of these differences is questionable, and may well be an underestimate, as it seems that many of the pupils with more severe levels of needs did not take part, especially in the Year 5 study. However, this is unlikely to affect the pattern of the results.

Home Variables

10.1.5 Mother's Education

Level of mother's education was significantly related to the progress made by their children between Year 2 and Year 5. Pupils whose mothers were educated to secondary school level and upwards made about 2 to 6 standardised score points more progress than pupils whose mothers' education had not reached that level (the amount of progress increased with increasing level of education). When all other factors were considered simultaneously this difference in amount of progress was reduced to about 1 to 3 standardised score points. Increase in maternal educational level is also statistically significant with a coefficient slightly under –1 standardised score point. At first sight, this negative coefficient appears surprising, but it is actually not. This apparently strange result arises because the explanatory variables relate to Year 5. Since the Year 2 and Year 5 background variables are so closely correlated, we could not include them both in the equation at the same time. Instead we included the Year 5 characteristics and any improvement in qualifications since Year 2. If a mother had a degree at Year 5, and had not improved her education since Year 2, then it would be reasonable to assume that she also had a degree at Year 2. If a mother had a degree in Year 5, and had gained higher education qualifications during the three years, she would have started without a degree in Year 2, and thus, on average, been of lower attainment during the three years than a mother who had been in the higher category the whole time. This effect disappeared after allowing for all other factors, such as father's occupation and education.

10.1.6 Father's Education

The level of education of pupils' fathers was significantly related to progress made between Year 2 and Year 5 when considered alone and alongside all other factors. Ignoring those with no formal schooling, which is quite a small category, the amount of progress made increased with increasing level of education. Those pupils whose fathers were educated to secondary level made around 2 standardised score points more progress, and those whose father studied at university made about 5 standardised score points more progress. These differences were reduced after taking account of other factors.

10.1.7 Mother's Occupation

When considered in exclusion of all the other factors, mothers' occupations were significantly related to the progress their child made. The amount of progress made increased with the increasing occupational scale. Pupils whose mothers were in the 'Semi-skilled, unskilled workers and labourers' category made about 2 standardised score points less progress than those categorised as 'Other', while pupils whose mothers were in the 'Professional' category made almost 3 standardised score points more progress. However, unlike the results of the English test, when all other factors were accounted for, the effect of maternal occupation on their children's progress was not statistically significant. This was probably because their level of education was also being accounted for.

10.1.8 Father's Occupation

Father's occupation was significantly related to the progress made by their children when considered alongside all other factors, and when allowing for Year 2 score only. Pupils whose fathers had a higher level of occupation made more progress. This additional progress ranged from around 2 to 7 standardised score points, in the model adjusted for prior attainment only. When all other factors were included, additional progress dropped to around 3 or 4 standardised score points.

School Variables

10.1.9 Number of Classes

The number of classes within a school in both Year 2 and Year 5 bore no relation to the progress made by pupils.

10.1.10 Type of School

Pupils made equivalent progress in Maltese irrespective of the type of school they attended (state or private).

10.1.11 Region

Pupils attending schools in different regions of Malta made equivalent progress.

10.2 English

Table 10.2 shows the results of the multilevel analyses for the English test, first with all the variables taken singly but adjusted only for prior attainment ('adjusted for pretest'), and then including all variables simultaneously ('adjusted').

Pupil Variables

10.2.1 Gender

As with the Maltese test, girls and boys made equivalent amounts of progress between Years 2 and 5.

10.2.2 Age

There was no statistically significant age effect.

10.2.3 First Language

Pupils whose first language was not Maltese made significantly more progress between Years 2 and 5 than their peers. These were pupils whose first language was English or who were bilingual and they made 2 or 3 standardised score points more progress.

10.2.4 Special Educational Needs

Pupils' level of Special Educational Needs (SEN) had a significant relationship with progress. Pupils with mild to moderate SEN made about 7 standardised score points less progress than pupils with no SEN, while pupils with severe to very severe SEN made 8 standardised score points less progress. If a pupil's level of SEN had increased or decreased since Year 2 their progress decreased or increased respectively, by 4 standardised score points.

Table 10.2: Multilevel Modelling Results for the English Test

			Unadjusted for pretest			Fully adjusted model		
		N	Coefficient	s.e.	Chi-square	Coefficient	s.e.	Chi-square
Pupil variables								
Prior Attainment in English	Standardised score in Year 2	4239	0.60	0.01	1849.8***	0.49	0.01	1129.5***
Sex	Boys	2108	0	–	0.1	0	–	0.1
	Girls	2131	0.10	0.34		0.09	0.33	
Age	In years and (completed) months	4239	-0.07	0.04	2.2	-0.09	0.04	4.2*
First Language	Maltese	3866	0	–	20.7***	0	–	7.6**
	English	373	3.16	0.69		1.90	0.69	
SEN	None	4072	0	–	107.7***	0	–	104.5***
	Mild to moderate	118	-7.76	1.04		-7.57	1.02	
	Severe to very severe	49	-8.64	1.63		-8.38	1.60	
	Change in level of SEN since Year 2	530	4.21	0.52		4.13	0.51	
Home variables								
Mother's Education	Other	134	0	–	118.5***	0	–	28.7***
	No formal schooling	12	-3.80	3.06		-3.45	3.26	
	Primary School	355	0.35	1.11		0.18	1.27	
	Secondary School	3049	2.86	0.98		1.43	1.14	
	Pre-university courses and vocational courses	391	6.74	1.11		3.46	1.28	
	University Education	298	7.92	1.17		4.53	1.37	
	Increase in mother's education since Year 2	685	-1.98	0.51		-1.55	0.51	

Father's Education	Other	209	0	–	106.9***	0	–	10.1
	No formal schooling	16	-1.59	2.62		-0.72	2.82	
	Primary School	444	0.89	0.89		0.19	1.10	
	Secondary School	2629	2.67	0.76		0.84	1.00	
	Pre-university courses and vocational courses	406	5.33	0.91		2.06	1.12	
	University Education	535	6.55	0.87		2.26	1.14	
Mother's Occupation	Other	3188	0	–	59.5***	0	–	16.4**
	Professional	210	3.21	0.74		0.19	0.84	
	Managerial and administrative	114	3.19	0.99		0.98	0.99	
	Higher clerical, skilled craftsmen, technicians	310	3.44	0.62		2.00	0.62	
	Skilled manual workers and foremen	140	1.60	0.88		1.67	0.86	
	Semi-skilled, unskilled workers, labourers	277	-1.23	0.65		-0.83	0.64	
Father's Occupation	Other	357	0	–	119.2***	0	–	31.0***
	Professional	314	6.53	0.84		2.92	1.00	
	Managerial and administrative	664	5.11	0.71		2.73	0.79	
	Higher clerical, skilled craftsmen, technicians	750	3.70	0.67		1.88	0.75	
	Skilled manual workers and foremen	1306	1.61	0.62		0.46	0.69	
	Semi-skilled, unskilled workers, labourers	848	0.73	0.65		-0.11	0.71	

Table 10.2: Multilevel Modelling Results for the English Test (continued)

			Unadjusted for pretest			Fully adjusted model		
		N	Coefficient	s.e.	Chi-square	Coefficient	s.e.	Chi-square
School variables								
No. of Year 5 Classes	1	439	0	–	2.9	0	–	5.6
	2	1157	-1.85	1.31		-3.05	1.38	
	3	889	-1.29	1.55		-2.08	1.66	
	4	577	-1.42	1.86		-3.30	2.02	
	5	725	-2.63	1.92		-3.18	2.16	
	6	118	-1.04	4.68		-2.69	4.44	
	7	155	-0.42	4.66		-1.80	4.97	
	9	179	0.76	4.65		-3.05	4.47	
No. of Year 2 Classes	1	495	0	–	7.2	0	–	9.1
	2	1234	0.83	0.99		1.99	1.07	
	3	879	-0.25	1.14		0.82	1.27	
	4	714	2.36	1.25		3.09	1.40	
	5	433	-0.56	1.48		0.16	1.61	
	6	248	0.60	1.77		1.20	1.86	
	7	151	2.40	2.69		4.00	3.06	
	8	85	3.14	1.83		3.89	1.93	
Type of School	State School	2772	0	–	8.5**	0	–	3.3
	Private School	1467	3.00	1.00		1.85	1.01	
Region	Inner Harbour	1090	0	–	6.5	0	–	4.3
	Outer Harbour	1214	1.64	1.35		2.34	1.34	
	South Eastern	576	-2.22	1.62		-0.06	1.57	
	Western	597	0.09	1.60		0.57	1.45	
	Northern	431	1.00	1.96		0.87	1.94	
	Gozo	331	1.83	1.56		1.69	1.47	

Home Variables

10.2.5 Mother's Education

For mothers educated up to secondary school and beyond, level of education was significantly related to their children's progress. When considered in absence of all other variables, pupils made between 3 and 7 standardised score points more progress than those with primary education only. This amount of additional progress was reduced to 2 to 5 standardised score points when all other variables were taken into account. Increase in maternal educational level was also statistically significant with a coefficient slightly under –2 standardised score points. At first sight, this result appears surprising, but it was actually not. This apparently strange result arises because the explanatory variables relate to Year 5. Since the Year 2 and Year 5 background variables are so closely correlated, we could not include them both in the equation at the same time. Instead we included the Year 5 characteristics and any improvement in qualifications since Year 2. If a mother had a degree at Year 5, and had not improved her education since Year 2, then it would be reasonable to assume that she also had a degree at Year 2. If a mother had a degree in Year 5, and had gained higher education qualifications during the three years, she would have started without a degree in Year 2. Thus, on average, she would have been of lower attainment during the three years than a mother who had been in the higher category the whole time.

10.2.6 Father's Education

Father's education was statistically significant in both models but the level of significance and the coefficients were less in the fully adjusted model.

10.2.7 Mother's Occupation

Pupils whose mothers were in the top three categories of the occupational scale made significantly more progress than their peers, by about 3 standardised score points. However, when all other variables were considered simultaneously, only pupils whose mothers were in the middle category 'higher clerical, skilled craftsmen and technicians', made more progress. Since mothers' level of education was already being taken into account, the effect of maternal occupation was reduced.

10.2.8 Father's Occupation

Father's occupation was significantly related to the progress made by their children. The amount of additional progress made increased with the occupational scale to as much as 6 standardised score points. However, when all other variables were taken into account, it was only the pupils whose fathers were in the top three categories that were making additional progress, of about 3 or 4 standardised score points.

School Variables

10.2.9 Number of Classes

As with the results for the Maltese test, pupils made equivalent progress irrespective of the number of classes in both Year 2 and Year 5.

10.2.10 Type of School

Unlike the results of the Maltese test where there was no discernible relationship between school type and progress made, pupils attending private schools made around 3 standardised score points more progress than those attending state schools. However, after adjusting for all other variables, school type bore no statistically significant relation to progress made by pupils.

10.2.11 Region

As with the results for the Maltese test, pupils attending schools in different regions of Malta all made equivalent progress. The

Table 10.3: Multilevel Modelling Results for the Maltese Test for State Schools Only

			Unadjusted for pretest			Fully adjusted model		
		N	Coefficient	s.e.	Chi-square	Coefficient	s.e.	Chi-square
Pupil variables								
Prior Attainment in Maltese	Standardised Score in Year 2	2772	0.63	0.01	1377.0***	0.52	0.02	849.6***
Sex	Boys	1432	0	–	2.7	0	–	2.4
	Girls	1340	0.70	0.43		0.64	0.41	
Age	In years and (completed) months	2772	-0.09	0.06	2.4	-0.10	0.06	3.0
First Language	Maltese	2720	0	–	1.1	0	–	0.0
	Not Maltese	52	1.61	1.58		0.01	1.52	
SEN	None	2673	0	–	119.5***	0	–	103.8***
	Mild to moderate	70	-7.49	1.45		-7.26	1.43	
	Severe to very severe	29	-10.45	2.28		-8.90	2.23	
	Change in level of SEN since Year 2	447	6.04	0.63		5.49	0.62	
Home variables								
Mother's Education	Other	85	0	–	79.2***	0	–	11.4
	No formal schooling	7	3.86	4.36		-3.40	4.96	
	Primary School	295	4.29	1.48		0.88	1.67	
	Secondary School	2111	6.38	1.34		1.72	1.53	
	Pre-university courses and vocational courses	151	11.16	1.65		3.92	1.85	
	University Education	123	12.54	1.74		4.47	2.03	
	Increase in mother's educationsince Year 2	345	-2.75	0.73		-1.56	0.71	

Table 10.3: Multilevel Modelling Results for the Maltese Test for State Schools Only (continued)

			Unadjusted for pretest			Fully adjusted model		
		N	Coefficient	s.e.	Chi-square	Coefficient	s.e.	Chi-square
Father's Education	Other	147	0	–	110.7***	0	–	18.8**
	No formal schooling	13	7.65	3.17		8.24	3.68	
	Primary School	378	5.22	1.11		3.71	1.37	
	Secondary School	1853	6.66	0.99		4.44	1.27	
	Pre-university courses and vocational courses	170	9.02	1.28		5.15	1.53	
	University Education	211	12.33	1.24		6.42	1.58	
Mother's Occupation	Other	294	0	–	47.0***	0	–	16.7**
	Professional	89	3.71	1.33		0.04	1.50	
	Managerial and administrative	214	7.99	2.14		3.71	2.12	
	Higher clerical, skilled craftsmen, technicians	471	4.08	0.99		2.40	0.99	
	Skilled manual workers and foremen	999	1.64	1.19		1.69	1.15	
	Semi-skilled, unskilled workers, labourers	705	-2.12	0.80		-1.79	0.77	
Father's Occupation	Other	2233	0	–	104.5***	0	–	23.9***
	Professional	72	10.49	1.36		5.13	1.55	
	Managerial and administrative	27	7.32	1.00		3.29	1.11	
	Higher clerical, skilled craftsmen, technicians	132	4.79	0.84		1.65	0.93	
	Skilled manual workers and foremen	90	2.63	0.75		0.21	0.83	
	Semi-skilled, unskilled workers, labourers	218	1.98	0.77		0.03	0.85	

School variables								
No. of Year 5 Classes	1	206	0	–	5.0	0	–	6.4
	2	532	-2.85	1.53		-3.40	1.80	
	3	502	-0.97	1.72		-1.53	2.06	
	4	427	-1.50	1.88		-1.13	2.44	
	5	653	-2.48	1.85		-4.07	2.66	
	6	118	-1.57	3.84		-4.75	4.03	
	7	155	-2.42	3.81		-2.61	4.67	
	9	179	1.81	3.80		-0.44	4.17	
No. of Year 2 Classes	1	188	0	–	2.5	0	–	1.5
	2	634	-1.67	1.33		1.10	1.63	
	3	478	-0.83	1.51		0.48	1.90	
	4	645	-0.20	1.48		1.60	1.87	
	5	349	-0.34	1.81		1.89	2.14	
	6	243	-0.98	2.01		1.57	2.32	
	7	151	-0.65	2.75		2.02	3.47	
	8	84	-0.08	2.09		1.46	2.38	
Type of School	Primary A/B	1466	0	–	0	0	–	0.3
	Primary C	1306	-0.13	1.17		0.92	1.73	
Region	Inner Harbour	338	0	–	11.1*	0	–	9.0
	Outer Harbour	872	3.55	1.50		3.90	1.54	
	South Eastern	530	2.59	1.60		2.66	1.49	
	Western	422	2.34	1.72		1.10	1.55	
	Northern	368	3.91	1.88		1.49	1.82	
	Gozo	242	5.55	1.69		3.93	1.51	

Table 10.4: Multilevel Modelling Results for the English Test for State Schools Only

			Unadjusted for pretest			Fully adjusted model		
		N	Coefficient	s.e.	Chi-square	Coefficient	s.e.	Chi-square
Pupil variables								
Prior Attainment in English	Standardised score in Year 2	2772	0.61	0.02	1262.0***	0.49	0.02	750.5***
Sex	Boys	1432	0	–	0.5	0	–	1.3
	Girls	1340	0.27	0.39		0.43	0.37	
Age	In years and (completed) months	2772	-0.09	0.05	2.6	-0.09	0.05	3.1
First Language	Maltese	2720	0	–	16.1***	0	–	12.9***
	English	52	5.80	1.44		5.00	1.39	
SEN	None	2673	0	–	91.8***	0	–	83.4***
	Mild to moderate	70	-6.69	1.34		-6.54	1.31	
	Severe to very severe	29	-7.29	2.11		-6.35	2.05	
	Change in level of SEN since Year 2	447	4.76	0.58		4.37	0.56	
Home variables								
Mother's Education	Other	85	0	–	111.2***	0	–	27.1***
	No formal schooling	7	-2.09	3.98		-2.43	4.54	
	Primary School	295	1.73	1.36		0.39	1.53	
	Secondary School	2111	4.50	1.24		2.14	1.40	
	Pre-university courses and vocational courses	151	9.91	1.52		4.81	1.70	
	University Education	123	11.74	1.60		6.20	1.86	
	Increase in mother's education since Year 2	345	-3.23	0.67		-2.32	0.66	

Father's Education	Other	147	0	–	104.4***	0	–	10.5
	No formal schooling	13	-1.55	2.91		-1.01	3.36	
	Primary School	378	2.08	1.03		0.53	1.25	
	Secondary School	1853	3.59	0.92		0.91	1.16	
	Pre-university courses and vocational courses	170	6.37	1.19		2.12	1.40	
	University Education	211	9.63	1.14		3.45	1.45	
Mother's Occupation	Other	294	0	–	62.6***	0	–	26.0***
	Professional	89	3.41	1.22		-0.84	1.37	
	Managerial and administrative	214	9.45	1.96		5.40	1.94	
	Higher clerical, skilled craftsmen, technicians	471	5.05	0.91		3.26	0.91	
	Skilled manual workers and foremen	999	1.82	1.09		1.86	1.05	
	Semi-skilled, unskilled workers, labourers	705	-0.99	0.74		-0.95	0.71	
Father's Occupation	Other	2233	0	–	97.2***	0	–	22.1***
	Professional	72	9.62	1.25		5.32	1.42	
	Managerial and administrative	27	5.56	0.93		2.53	1.01	
	Higher clerical, skilled craftsmen, technicians	132	4.18	0.78		2.28	0.85	
	Skilled manual workers and foremen	90	1.89	0.69		0.78	0.76	
	Semi-skilled, unskilled workers, labourers	218	1.26	0.71		0.59	0.78	

Table 10.4: Multilevel Modelling Results for the English Test for State Schools Only (continued)

			Unadjusted for pretest			Fully adjusted model		
		N	Coefficient	s.e.	Chi-square	Coefficient	s.e.	Chi-square
School variables								
No. of Year 5 Classes	1	206	0	–	9.6	0	–	16.9*
	2	532	-4.86	1.63		-6.34	1.80	
	3	502	-1.94	1.87		-4.03	2.07	
	4	427	-2.87	2.06		-7.23	2.49	
	5	653	-3.20	2.04		-8.54	2.76	
	6	118	-1.37	4.34		-8.19	4.29	
	7	155	-0.74	4.31		-6.37	4.78	
	9	179	0.48	4.30		-8.86	4.48	
No. of Year 2 Classes	1	188	0	–	6.5	0	–	6.5
	2	634	-1.25	1.35		2.78	1.55	
	3	478	-1.08	1.54		1.63	1.80	
	4	645	1.22	1.52		3.51	1.78	
	5	349	-0.93	1.84		2.36	2.04	
	6	243	-0.12	2.01		2.46	2.19	
	7	151	1.74	2.77		4.20	3.19	
	8	84	2.13	2.03		4.66	2.22	
Type of School	Primary A/B	1466	0	–	2.6	0	–	3.6
	Primary C	1306	-2.14	1.32		-3.52	1.85	
Region	Inner Harbour	338	0	–	16.1**	0	–	10.1
	Outer Harbour	872	4.07	1.66		3.08	1.65	
	South Eastern	530	1.21	1.76		0.80	1.58	
	Western	422	3.14	1.90		2.28	1.67	
	Northern	368	3.72	2.08		2.29	1.95	
	Gozo	242	7.11	1.83		4.75	1.60	

differences in progress between regions were not statistically significant either in the fully adjusted or partially adjusted analyses.

As a follow-up to these findings, it was noted that the region variable was not really relevant to church and independent schools, since they typically drew their pupils from a wide catchment area. For this reason, the analyses were repeated, confining them to pupils in state schools only. The results are shown in Tables 10.3 and 10.4. It can be seen that when the analyses were confined to state schools, the differences were statistically significant in both partially adjusted and adjusted analyses, with Gozo, and to a lesser extent Outer Harbour, outperforming Inner Harbour. These results are positive for Gozo, which was behind at Year 2, but must be less so for Inner Harbour.

10.3 School-Level Results

As well as exploring the relationships that existed between the various factors and pupils' progress between Years 2 and 5, it was of interest to consider how a school's overall progress differed from the average or from what would be expected. Multilevel modelling allowed us to examine the differential performance of schools. This was achieved by looking at the difference between each school's performance and what would be expected. This difference between actual and expected is known as a *'residual'*.

Pupils' performance was assessed at a single time point in an attempt to measure their ability. However, pupils were likely to perform differently on a test on one day than they could do the day after. As with any measurement, assessment of their ability was subject to an element of variation, known as '*random error*'. The statistical analysis used in this investigation made allowance for this by quoting not only an average value, but also a range within which this average feasibly lay.

Below are graphs of school-level residuals. 'Average' progress is denoted by zero. Schools have been sorted in order of increasing progress. Schools to the left-hand side of the graph and below the zero line, made less than average progress. Schools to the right-hand side of the graph and above the zero line, made more than average progress. Also indicated on the graphs is each school's feasible range (or *'confidence interval'*). If a school's confidence interval crosses the zero line, then the progress made cannot be said to have been any different from the average or from expectation. Only if a school's confidence interval lies wholly above or below the zero line can we say that their progress was greater or less, respectively, than average.

Two sets of three graphs are shown below, the first three for Maltese, and the second three for English. The first graph shows the 'raw' or unadjusted residuals for each school, and gives an impression of how much below or above the average in the whole population they were. A school on the extreme right of this graph would contain pupils who read very well, while a school on the extreme left would contain pupils who did less well. The second graph looks at the progress made by pupils over the period between and takes account of the fact that not all pupils started at the same level of attainment. If all pupils had made exactly the same progress over the period, then the graph would be completely flat. A school on the extreme right of this graph would have pupils who had made very good progress over the period. In many cases they were schools which were performing well in reading at Year 5, but this is not necessarily the case. It could be that the pupils had been relatively unsuccessful at Year 2, but had 'caught up' between then and Year 5. The third graph takes account of the fact that it is not equally easy to teach all pupils, and makes allowance for factors that have been found to influence educational attainment. A school on the extreme right of the graph could be a school which performed well in reading at Year 5, but it could also be a school in relatively deprived circumstances that had managed to make average progress.

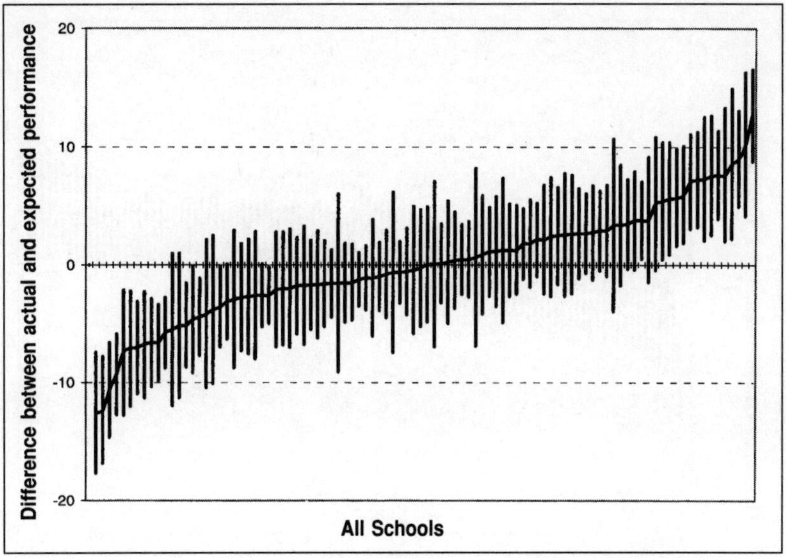

Figure 10.1: Schools in order of completely unadjusted Year 5 Maltese score residuals.

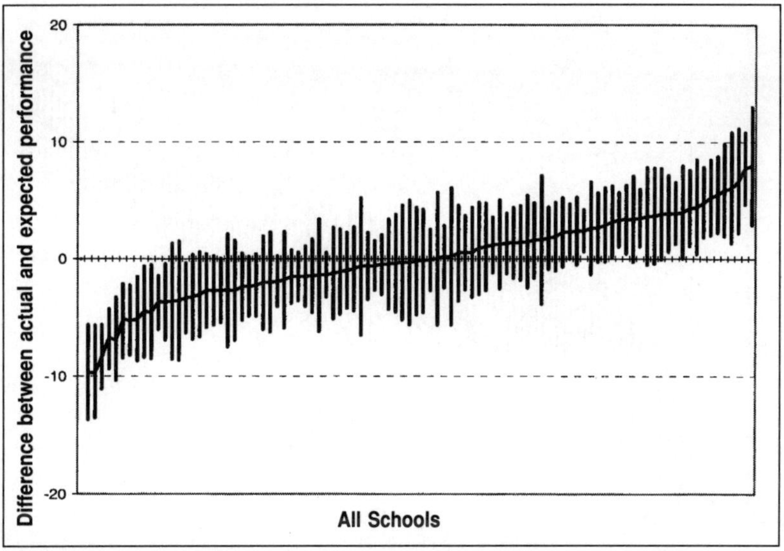

Figure 10.2: Schools in order of Year 5 Maltese score residuals adjusted for prior attainment only.

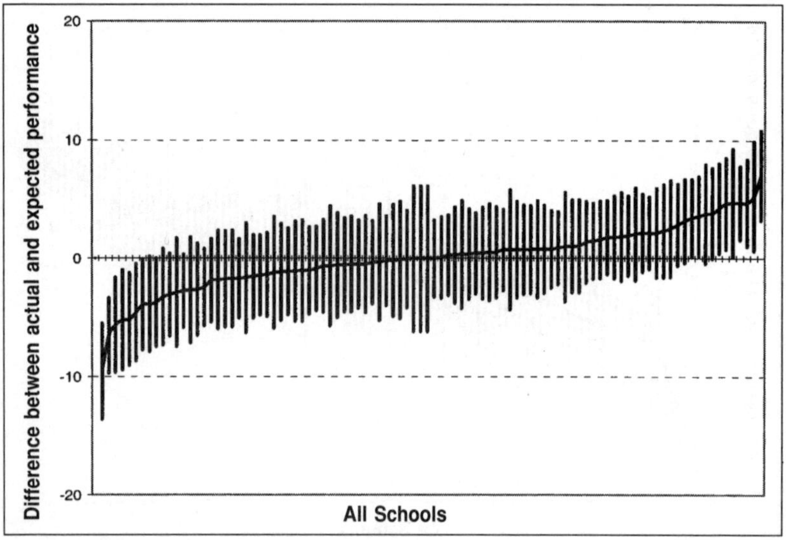

Figure 10.3: Schools in order of adjusted Year 5 Maltese score residuals.

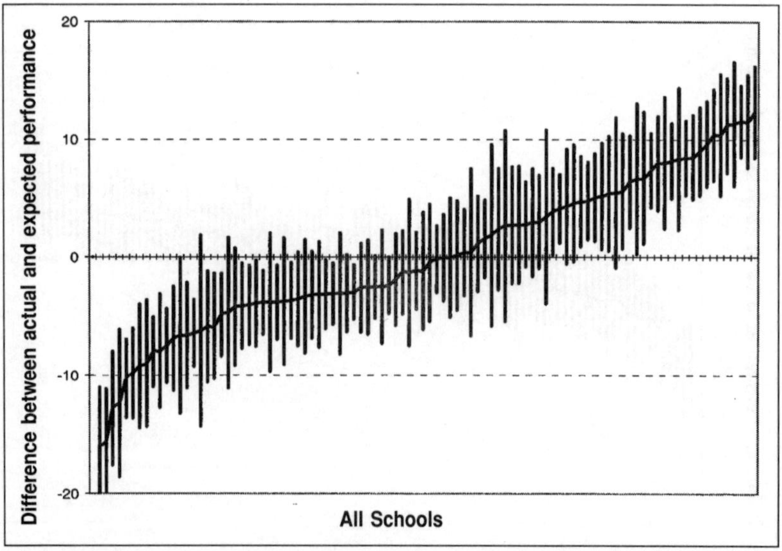

Figure 10.4: Schools in order of completely unadjusted Year 5 English score residuals.

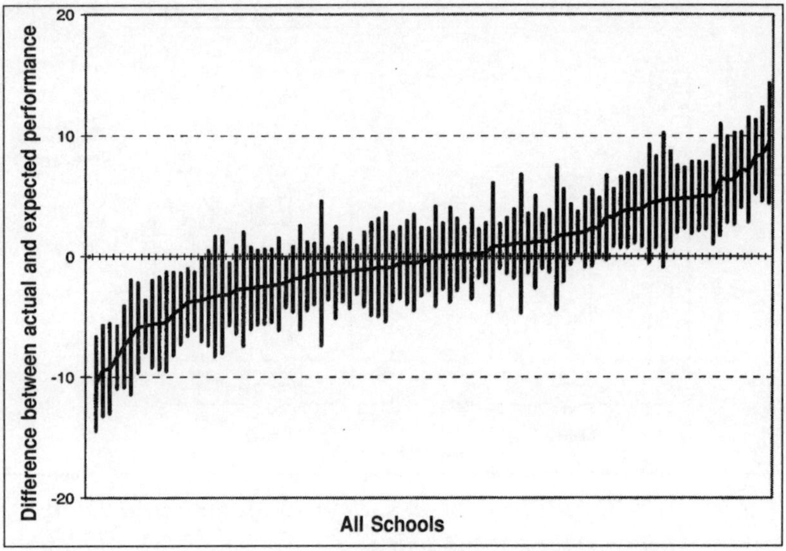

Figure 10.5: Schools in order of Year 5 English score residuals adjusted for prior attainment only.

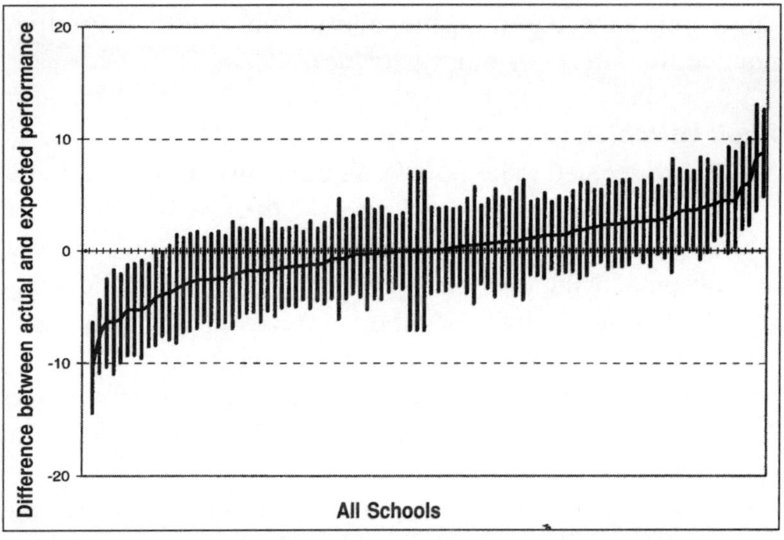

Figure 10.6: Schools in order of adjusted Year 5 English score residuals.

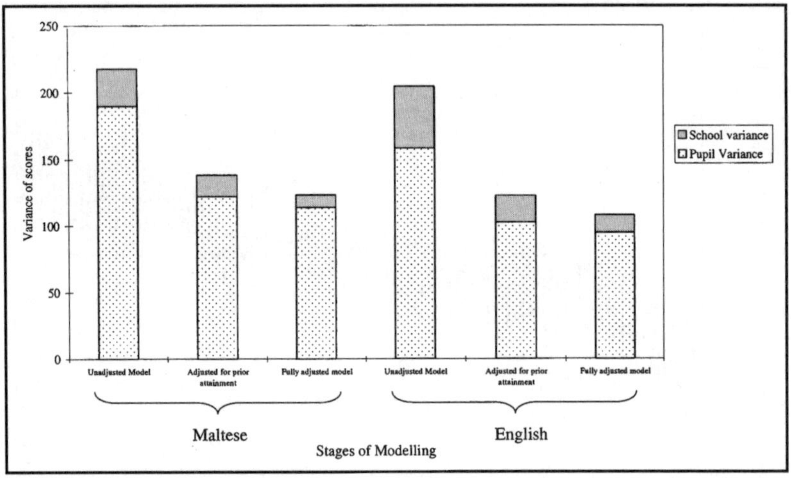

Figure 10.7: Variance of scores for both Maltese and English at the various stages of modelling.

10.4 Summary

This summary is based on the adjusted analyses because they remove the effects of other variables.

Pupil Variables

- There seemed to be no differences between boys and girls in the amount of progress over the three years. This is not to say that girls were not ahead - in fact the analyses accompanying the Year 5 Literacy Study made it clear that they were- simply that they were maintaining the gap, neither drawing away, nor allowing it to close.
- There were no differences in the amount of progress over the three years between older and younger pupils in Maltese.
- Comparing like with like, pupils for whom Maltese was the first language on average made more progress in Maltese over the three years than those for whom it was not.

Conversely pupils for whom Maltese was not the first language (mainly English-speaking, but a few bilingual) made on average more progress in English over the three years than those for whom Maltese was the first language.

- Pupils with special educational needs made less progress than those without, and the more severe the assessed category, the less progress was made. Pupils who were assessed as having special needs at one time point (either Year 2 or Year 5), made more progress than those who were assessed as having special needs at both. Those who were SEN in Year 2 but not in Year 5 improved, while those who were not SEN in Year 2 but became SEN in Year 5 declined.

Home Variables

- Both mother's education and father's education had an effect on progress for Year 2 and Year 5. The more education a parent had, the more progress the child made. This was observed both for the effect of the parental education when considered on its own, and after allowing for all other factors, so these were clearly important and independently acting effects. Changes in mother's level of education had an effect over and above that of mother's education on its own, so that a child whose mother had only attained a particular educational level during the period did not make quite so much progress as a child whose mother had been at that level the whole period. Changes in father's education did not have a comparable impact.
- Parental occupation, especially the father's, was generally taken as an indication of the material and cultural resources available in the home to promote a child's education. The social status of the father's occupation was strongly related to the progress a pupil made over the period, in the order:

professional, managerial and administrative, skilled craftsmen and higher clerical, skilled manual workers, semi- and unskilled workers, no employed father (mainly unemployed). There appeared to be no observable effect of the father changing his job.

- Mother's occupation was also related to the child's progress in Maltese over the period, though the relationship was less strong, largely because fewer mothers were in paid employment. The largest group by far was that of mothers not in paid employment. They were a very mixed group, married to fathers who came from all social classes, and as such the mean progress of their children was quite close to that of the population as a whole, including skilled manual workers and semi- and unskilled manual workers. Due to the very small number of mothers who were working at the Year 2 stage, no information was collected on mother's employment then, and so it was not possible to assess the effect of a mother changing her occupation.

School Variables

- There was no evidence that size of school, as measured by number of classes, either at Year 2 or Year 5, was related to pupil progress.
- There was no difference in progress in Maltese between pupils in the different types of school they attended (state, private church or private independent). In contrast pupils attending private schools (church or independent) made significantly more progress in English than those attending state schools. Private school pupils made around 3 standardised score points more progress. However, when adjusting for all other variables, school type did not have a statistically significant relation to progress made by pupils. The great majority of pupils who spoke English as their first language attended private schools, and the additional

progress in these schools may be largely due to the characteristics of the pupils and their families.

- There were some differences between regions of the country, with the Inner Harbour area making less progress. However, by contrast to the findings for the two literacy studies on their own, differences in progress between the regions were not statistically significant for progress. When confining the analysis to state schools, since the catchment areas for private (church and independent) schools were less well-defined, we found that pupils in the Inner Harbour region made less progress, and the pupils in Gozo made more. This must be heartening for Gozo schools, since pupils in Gozo performed less well than other areas at Year 2, and it appears that they are catching up. It was less encouraging for Inner Harbour, which was behind at Year 2, but made less progress.

Chapter 11

The Effects of Streaming

11.1 Introduction

Over the age range of this study, pupils in state schools in Malta are streamed at the beginning of Year 5 based on the marks attained in the annual exams at the end of Year 4, and the streams are re-ordered at the beginning of Year 6. For this reason and on strong recommendation from heads of schools who attended the literacy feedback sessions (see Section Three of this study) it was decided to look specifically at the effect of streaming on pupils' performance and progress.

In general, pupils in streamed classes do rather worse overall than those in unstreamed classes: in Maltese this difference is not statistically significant, but in English pupils in streamed schools make between three and four standardised score points less progress than those in unstreamed schools. However by this stage, Year 5, the streaming process has not widened the gap between the more and less successful pupils.

11.2 Methods of Organising Pupils within Schools

Methods of organising pupils within a school vary from country to country and frequently from school to school within a country. One type is a selective school system, in which pupils are allocated to a school, frequently at age 11, and while it is possible to transfer between different types of school at a later age, in practice most pupils remain for the rest of their school career within the school to which they were first allocated.

The other type is the comprehensive system, under which all pupils within an area attend a single school. Within schools, too, there is a range of segregation. At one extreme, there are 'banded' schools, in which pupils are allocated to one of a number of bands within the year group, each of these bands containing a number of classes. This behaves in some ways as if a number of selective schools were located within the same building. At the other extreme is a mixed ability grouping system in which the aim is not to differentiate between classes on ability: indeed some mixed ability arrangements have deliberately managed the allocation of pupils to classes with the aim of making all classes of comparable ability. Within these two extremes, pupils may be **streamed**, i.e. allocated to a single class for all their lessons on the basis of their ability, or **setted**, i.e. allocated to a class on ability for each subject. Some schools will set pupils on all subjects, others just on English and Mathematics.

Policies vary between systems, and, within systems, over time. Thus in the United Kingdom in the 1950s, pupils were allocated to grammar, secondary modern or technical schools on the basis of a test taken at age 11, and then classes were streamed within these schools. At present, with parental choice, and the effects of surviving grammar schools, and a small but in many areas independent sector, there is a very wide range of arrangements between areas. Probably the most common arrangement is to have a comprehensive school taking the preponderance of pupils in an area, and within such a school pupils are setted for English and Mathematics, (Davies et al., 2003).

In Malta, state schools are streamed from the beginning of year 5, so that the pupils in this study will have been in mixed ability classes at the start of the study (year 2), and, except for small schools, in streamed classes by the end of the study (year 5).

There is always considerable interest in the effect of streaming pupils within a school, not just in Malta, but worldwide. Arguments for and against streaming vary. Those in favour point largely to organisational benefits. They argue that it is much easier for teachers to organise their lessons if all pupils are of comparable ability, and that brighter pupils are encouraged by high attaining classmates (compositional effects), while the less academic are not put off by being constantly at the tail, (Hutchison, 2003). On the other hand, those against emphasise social as much as educational benefits. They argue that the normal selection ages, such as 11 or even earlier, as in the case of Malta, are too soon for ability to settle down and that many pupils will be labelled as unsuccessful, despite the fact that they might still be able to develop substantially. They also argue that compositional effects are a zero-sum game that benefits high ability pupils by having aspirational classmates. However, these benefits are balanced by losses for those in the lower streams, who do not have the benefit of education-friendly peers (Opdenakker and Van Damme, 2001). Also, it is argued, those in the lower streams are effectively 'written off' by being told at an early age that they are not going to be academically successful.

In view of the arrangement that all state schools in Malta are streamed from Year 5, there is not much opportunity to investigate the effect of streaming, with one exception. One type of school cannot be streamed, that is schools with only one class in a year. We thus compare unstreamed schools, i.e. those with only one class per year, against those with two or more. The analyses reported below consider three questions:

- Is there any overall effect on attainment of being in a streamed or unstreamed class?
- Is there an effect on equity of being in streamed on unstreamed classes? Is progress more differentiated in streamed classes?
- If there are any effects, do they hold equally for Maltese and English?

11.3 Findings

First, we consider the effect of streaming on overall attainment. Tables 11.1 and 11.2 show the difference between progress in

Table 11.1: The Effect of Streaming on Progress

			Unadjusted for pretest			Fully Adjusted model		
		N	Coefficient	s.e.	Chi-square	Coefficient	s.e.	Chi-square
Maltese	Unstreamed	206	0			0		
	Streamed	2566	–2.00	1.37	2.09	–1.95	1.2	2.6
English	Unstreamed	206	0			0		
	Streamed	2566	–3.36	1.49	4.9*	–3.67	1.25	8.1**

Table 11.2: The Effect of Streaming on Equity in Progress

			Unadjusted for pretest			Fully Adjusted model		
		N	Coefficient	s.e.	Chi-square	Coefficient	s.e.	Chi-square
Maltese	Unstreamed	206	0			0		0.04
	Streamed	2566	–0.01	0.06	0.04	–0.01	0.06	
English	Unstreamed	206	0			0		
	Streamed	2566	–0.05	0.07	0.5	0.07	0.07	1.1

streamed and unstreamed classes, first on its own, and second, after allowing for other factors that might influence progress. Analyses are confined to state schools, since there is no information about private schools. We show only the results for the streaming variable, as the other effects are comparable to those for the state schools reported earlier in tables 10.3 and 10.4. The first part of each table deals with the question of whether there is any overall effect of streaming. The results suggest that pupils in streamed classes do rather worse overall than those in unstreamed. In Maltese this difference is not statistically significant, but in English, pupils in streamed schools make between three and four standardised score points less progress than those in unstreamed schools. However there is no identifiable effect on the slope. That is to say that at this stage the streaming process has not widened the gap between the more and less successful pupils.

However, could this simply be an effect of small schools? This is unlikely, because research has suggested that pupils in smaller schools do not in fact do any better, and also because there appears not to be any trend showing that a larger number of classes per year in a school, results in lower attainment. However it is questionable whether this could be applied within the Maltese context. By carrying out further analysis on the effects of streaming, it was possible to come up with the following results.

As was previously explained, pupils in large schools were streamed in Year 5, while in Year 2 they were unstreamed. On the other hand, pupils in small schools were unstreamed in both Year 2 and Year 5 owing to the fact that there was only one class per year. Following the recommendation of Kenny (1975), the analysis focused on whether the gap in attainment widened or narrowed in the period from Year 2 to Year 5. If it has changed, then this suggests an effect of streaming versus mixed ability. This entails comparing the two cross-sectional studies conducted in 1999 on all Year 2 pupils and in 2002 on all Year 5 pupils. The number of classes per school appears to have remained relatively constant between Year 2 and Year 5. Thus, one can say that if there is a change in relative performance of the two groups between Year 2 and Year 5, this suggests that the main change over the period between the two groups, namely the introduction of streaming, is likely to be the cause of this change.

Table 11.3 shows the comparison between streamed and unstreamed schools at Year 2 and Year 5, for English and Maltese.

Table 11.3: Differences in Attainment between Small Schools and Large Schools

	Score	SD	Score	SD	P-value
Year 2	**Small Schools (Unstreamed)**		**Large Schools (Unstreamed)**		
Maltese	102	1.03	102.5	0.29	0.38
English	99.6	0.93	98.5	0.26	0.32
Year 5	**Small Schools (Unstreamed)**		**Large Schools (Streamed)**		
Maltese	101.4	1.04	99.8	0.29	0.14
English	100.2	0.97	96.6	0.26	0.003
Change					
Maltese	-0.25	1.02	-2.65	0.25	0.02
English	0.56	1.08	-1.88	0.24	0.01

Note: Small schools comprise those schools with only one class per year. Large schools comprise those schools with 2 or more classes per year.

The first part of the table shows the Year 2 results, the second part shows the Year 5 results, while the third part of the table shows the changes in standardised scores between Year 2 and Year 5. Looking at the first two parts of the table, we see that there is no statistically significant difference in Maltese at either age. For English, on the other hand, while there is still no statistically significant difference at Year 2, there is one, in favour of small schools at Year 5. This suggests that streaming results in lower attainment in English but not in Maltese. However, it is not enough to look at the attainment of pupils in Maltese and English, in small and large schools at the 2 time points separately. It is important to measure the effects from Year 2 to Year 5.

The third part of the table shows the differences in standardised scores from Year 2 to Year 5 for the two groups in both Maltese and English. This shows clearly that streaming does in fact result in pupils achieving lower scores in both Maltese and English when taking the 3-year period, from 1999 to 2002, into consideration. One possible explanation for this is that pupils in streamed schools have experienced a fair degree of upheaval in changing from unstreamed to streamed, and that this has taken place relatively recently, especially since most schools shake up their streams every year. This could mean that pupils in streamed schools may be achieving lower scores not due to the effects of streaming *per se*, but more so as a result of the upheaval and changes involved.

Chapter 12

Implications and Recommendations

12.1 Implications

The Literacy Unit of the University of Malta and the Education Division of Malta, in co-operation with the National Foundation for Educational Research in England and Wales and the University of Sheffield, have carried out studies of literacy in Maltese and English in Maltese schools in Year 2 in 1999, and in Year 5 in 2002. The results of these studies have been reported in Mifsud et al. 2000, and in Section One of this publication. Since the same pupils were involved on both occasions, it has been possible to match the results from the two studies, and conduct a value added study. This study has compared the progress of pupils in different schools from Year 2 to Year 5. It has investigated the factors that would affect progress, and used the results from this to estimate progress scores for schools.

From the detailed findings, we were able to draw up two profiles, describing pupils who were likely to make the most progress, and those who were likely to make the least:

- most progress: pupils who spoke the language tested as a first language, with highly educated parents (university or pre-university) in professional occupations. For the English language, pupils at private (church or independent) schools made more progress.
- least progress: pupils who did not speak the language tested as a first language, with parents with little or no formal education, with mothers in semi- or unskilled work, and fathers in semi- or unskilled work, receiving state benefits, or absent.

There were differences between schools, but these were smaller after making allowance for the factors found to be of importance in predicting progress. Differences in English were larger than differences in Maltese. This was to be expected, and in line with research elsewhere, since the large preponderance of pupils speak Maltese as a first language at home, so the effect of schools is proportionately larger.

In the recommendations arising from the Year 2 Literacy Study, concern was expressed about the difference in literacy performance between boys and girls. It is reassuring that this gap has not widened noticeably.

Poor performance in literacy is something that materially handicaps citizens in modern society. Furthermore, it is not something that pupils, in general, will 'grow out of' as they get older, and the results of this study confirm this. Over half of those in the lowest fifth in reading ability in Maltese at Year 2 are still in the lowest fifth at Year 5.

As a new member of the European Union, Malta will experience a time of great opportunity, but also of great challenge. It is likely to be a time of surprisingly rapid change and overturning of assumptions. It will be vital to utilize and build on the islands' strengths. It will become increasingly important for the population to be fluent in one of the official EU languages, and English is the obvious candidate, given Malta's already excellent record in teaching English. While not de-emphasising the Maltese language in any way, the education system in Malta might wish to put an increased emphasis on the learning and use of English.

12.2 Methods for Improving Literacy Skills

Methods for improving reading have been categorised into three target groups or 'waves':

- Wave 1 refers to reading enhancement schemes, such as the Literacy Hour, which aim to improve the literacy of the entire population.

- Wave 2 refers to schemes which target pupils who, though not considered as having special educational needs, are nonetheless having problems with literacy, but can be expected to 'catch up' with their peers as a result of the intervention.
- Wave 3 refers to schemes targetted at pupils who have special educational needs.

A National Literacy Hour scheme was implemented in the UK, in which all pupils at the relevant stage had an hour of literacy training in the morning, and pupils' parents were strongly encouraged to take part. A comparable scheme, with a Maltese emphasis, could be implemented in Malta.

Schemes to boost the performance of slow readers have recently been reviewed by Brooks (2003). These relate to schemes in Britain, but it is likely that the system in Malta is sufficiently similar so that the findings are relevant, and this could be used as a source to select a scheme.

The continuing underperformance of the Inner Harbour area must be of concern, and it may be that this is largely due to a lack of family resources. Family Literacy schemes offer parents the opportunity to improve their own literacy skills with the aim of helping their children's progress. These have been investigated in the UK and elsewhere, and found to be highly effective, both in the short term and the medium term, (Brooks et al., 1996 and Brooks et al., 1997). While such schemes have been suggested in the context of improving literacy in the English language, they would be equally applicable, to the Maltese language.

Boys start at a lower attainment point in literacy in Year 2 than do girls, and this difference is maintained over the period Year 2 to Year 5. As with the population as a whole, it would be desirable to intervene at an early stage (before Year 2) to ensure that boys are not allowed to fall behind in literacy. Some schools may be more successful than others in doing this, and it would be of interest to investigate the characteristics of schools where such gender differences are relatively small.

Two points arose during individual discussions with schools (see Section Three of this publication), which are worthy of note. First, that qualified head teacher candidates are allocated to primary or secondary schools as the vacancies arise, regardless of the previous or current experience of the teachers themselves. This policy does not take account of the very different and specialised needs of each sector, and cannot be in the best interests of either teachers or schools. Second, there seems to be a tendency, in the absence of other information, to quote the results of examinations for entry into junior lyceums as a measure of a school's success. Such a pattern must lead to schools directing resources and attention to the more fortunate, and most likely to be successful, and away from those who perhaps need most support. A value added approach would help to direct attention to the whole school, and not just to the most academically successful.

12.3 Recommendations

- The results for each school from this study can form the basis of a value added study, and it is recommended that confidential individual school reports are produced. (This has taken place already.)
- We recommend that the research team offer each school the opportunity to discuss their own individual school report, and highlight their areas of strengths and weaknesses. (This has taken place already.)
- Schools should be offered an opportunity of some kind of in-service training to discuss what actions they could take to improve perceived shortcomings.
- With entry into the EU, the teaching and learning of English in schools should become a greater priority.

- Linguistic skills of pupils as a whole should be nurtured by introducing a Literacy Hour in schools at Year 1.
- Pupils should be tested at the beginning of Year 2, perhaps using the tests devised for the Year 2 Literacy Study. Special programmes should be initiated to help ensure that less successful readers, those with a standardized score of less than 85, are not left behind. A number of possible schemes for this would be possible, and examples of ones that have 'worked' are given in *What Works for Children with Literacy Difficulties* (Brooks, 2003). Some of the more successful should be considered
- The possibility of introducing a Family Literacy scheme should be considered to help the performance of pupils in the Inner Harbour area.
- The Value Added data set constructed for this study is an important potential source of information about the schools. Further analysis should be carried out on the Value Added data set to look at such questions as, for example, which schools have done better in preventing boys from falling behind in literacy, and what are the characteristics of these schools.
- We feel that the policy of allocating head teachers to primary or secondary schools, regardless of the sector they are currently teaching in, is not necessarily in the best interest of schools or teachers, and suggest that this policy might be reconsidered.
- A few case studies should be conducted in order to focus on particular aspects. It is necessary to look at key factors that might be influencing the pupils' rate of achievement such as, banding/ setting/ streaming, traditional effectiveness, interconnectedness, the school's ethos and culture, the size of the school, state as opposed to private schools, etc. and to investigate these issues.
- It is necessary to strengthen the School Improvement and Effectiveness services.

Section Three

Using Value Added Data For School Improvement

Introduction

One of the recommendations that emerged from the value added study was to develop an individual report for each school and for the research team to offer each school the opportunity to discuss their own individual school report and highlight their areas of strengths and weaknesses.

The 99 primary schools in Malta, included in the Year 5 and Value Added studies, were offered feedback by the Literacy Unit of the University of Malta, in collaboration with the National Foundation for Educational Research of England and Wales (NFER), and the Education Division of Malta. The significance of such value added studies and the way in which to interpret individual reports was discussed with schools.

In this section we are presenting a model of the individual report given to every school. Each school report was based on the data gathered from that particular school during the two National Literacy Surveys held in 1999 and 2002. Apart from the report, a general discussion was held for heads of schools. The main issues that were dealt with are presented in this section, after the model school report.

Chapter 13

The Value Added School Report Model

13.1 Introduction

This chapter presents a model of the individual school report given to all schools during a series of seminars organized specifically to give feedback to the heads of the 99 primary schools that were involved in both national surveys (1999, 2002).

Unlike the main report, which is general, this confidential report summarises the main findings as they relate to an individual school. It also provides some detailed explanations of value added data and practical guidance on how the school might be able to use the findings to assist with processes of school improvement.

The tables and figures provide detailed value added data, which are a truer reflection of the school's achievement than 'raw' data or test results. The tables and figures are presented together with guidance notes, so as to maximise understanding of the data and to assist schools to think about what action they might take as a result of these findings.

In order to assist schools when interpreting the report, a glossary of technical terms was included with the report (see Annex 1).

13.2 Analysing the Results

Table 13.1 compares the particular school's average test results (first two columns) with those for all the schools that participated in the study (second two columns). The average test scores for both Year 2 and Year 5 English and Maltese tests are provided.

The explanation below the tables summarises the school's results; both as raw, unadjusted data and after adjustments have been made to take account of a number of pupil background variables. These variables are listed below.

Pupil Variables Used in the Adjustment:
Pupils' Year 2 standardised score
Boys/girls
Age
SEN
First Language
Father's and Mother's Occupation
Father's and Mother's Education

Table 13.1: Results of Test Data for Both the Year 2 and Year 5 English and Maltese Tests

	Model School		All Schools	
	School Average	Total students	Overall Average	Total students
Year 5 (2002) English Standardised Score	90.9	108	100.0	5394
Year 5 (2002) Maltese Standardised Score	94.1	108	99.9	5358
Year 2 (1999) English Standardised Score	87.2	106	102.0	5038
Year 2 (1999) Maltese Standardised Score	91.5	106	102.8	5028

Summary of Value Added Analysis

Based on unadjusted residuals (raw results), in the case of this particular school, the school's performance in both the English and the Maltese tests was below average.

After adjusting for prior attainment and pupil background variables the school's performance on both the English and Maltese tests was not significantly different from the national average.

The adjusted values in Table 13.2 represent the differences between the actual performance indicators for the school and those 'expected', taking into account the given background

Table 13.2: Year 5 Unadjusted and Adjusted Test Results for English and Maltese

	English Score	Maltese Score
Unadjusted	✘	✘
Average	–7.93	–5.10
Upper limit	–3.30	–0.40
Lower limit	–12.56	–9.81
Adjusted for pupil data	≈≈≈	≈≈≈
Average	1.57	1.84
Upper limit	4.10	4.63
Lower limit	–0.97	–0.95

Key to symbols:
✘ Performance significantly below 'expected' values
≈≈≈ Performance not significantly different from 'expected' values
✓ Performance significantly above 'expected' values

variables. The 'lower limit' and 'upper limit' values represent the range within which 95% of the school's 'true' performance lies.

Table 13.2 gives a more visual representation of the school's average results in relation to other schools. Most schools will find that they have a ≈≈≈ symbol, which means that their average performance is not significantly different from what would be expected. A ✓ means a performance significantly better than expected and a ✘ means a performance significantly below than expected.

The adjusted values in Table 13.2 and Figure 13.1 represent the differences between the actual performance indicators for the school and those 'expected', taking into account the given background variables. Table 13.2 shows the exact values and statistical significance information. Figure 13.1 uses the information from Table 13.2 in the form of bar charts. This makes it easier to see the extent of any positive or negative differences between actual and expected scores in English and Maltese.

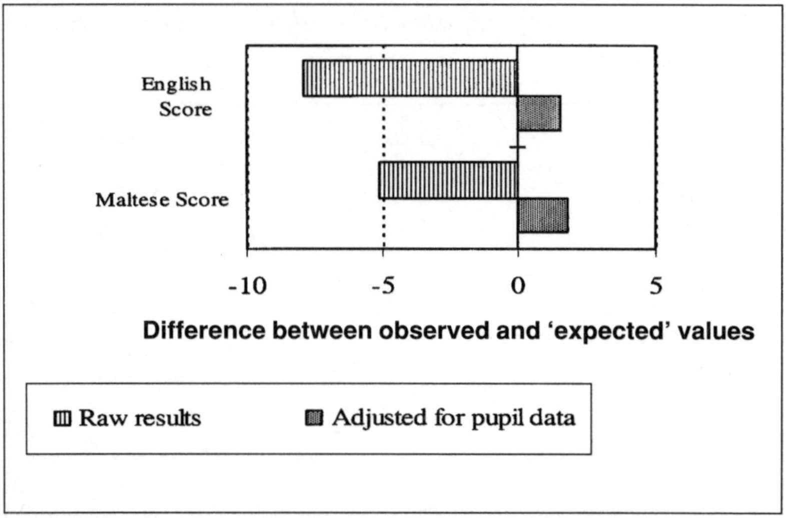

Figure 13.1: Year 5 unadjusted and adjusted test results for English and Maltese.

Analysis of Pupils' Performance

In Figure 13.2, the standardised scores each pupil obtained in the English test in Year 2 (1999) are plotted against their English test standardised scores for Year 5 (2002).

Figure 13.2 is a scatterplot. Symbols are used to represent individual pupils. This diagram shows how individual pupils, or particular groups of pupils, have performed in English over the three-year period. For example, one can see what proportion of pupils are above the 50th percentile line or how boys and girls performed or whether there are any groups of pupils who have underachieved or who have performed particularly well.

The plotted lines are derived from data from all schools in Malta. Nationally, one would expect about half of the pupils to fall above and half below the 50th percentile line. Similarly, 25% of the pupils would be expected to lie below the 25th percentile, and 75% above. Similar comments apply to the other percentile lines.

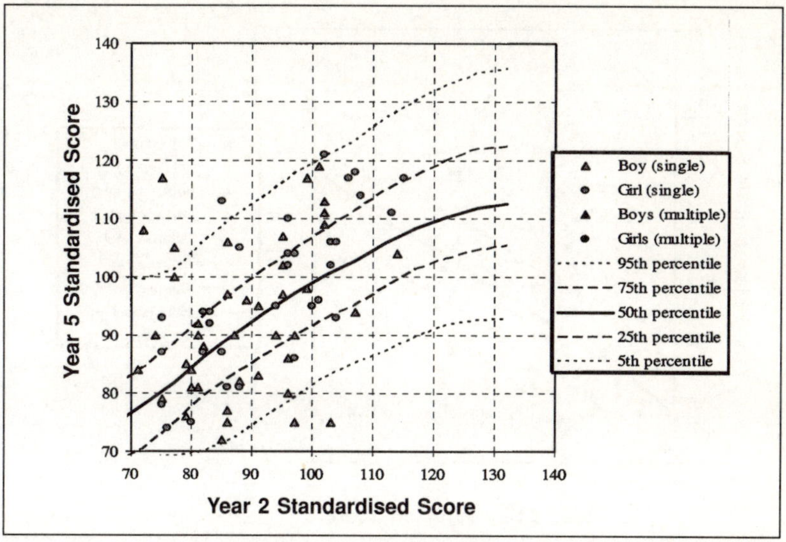

Figure 13.2: Pupils' Year 5 standardised scores in relation to their Year 2 standardised scores in English.

In Figure 13.3, the standardised scores each pupil obtained in the Maltese test in Year 2 (1999) are plotted against their Maltese standardised score for Year 5 (2002). This diagram is also a scatterplot as in Figure 13.2 above but is plotted for the Maltese standardised test scores.

The lines plotted are derived from data from all schools in Malta. Nationally, one would expect about half of the pupils to fall above and half below the 50th percentile line. Similarly, 25% of the pupils would be expected to lie below the 25th percentile, and 75% above. Similar comments apply to the other percentile lines.

Table 13.3 looks at how particular background variables impact upon the pupils in that particular school. For a range of background variables the table provides a school mean (or average) and the national mean. This enables the school to see whether its pupils (with particular background characteristics) have done better than expected in English compared with pupils

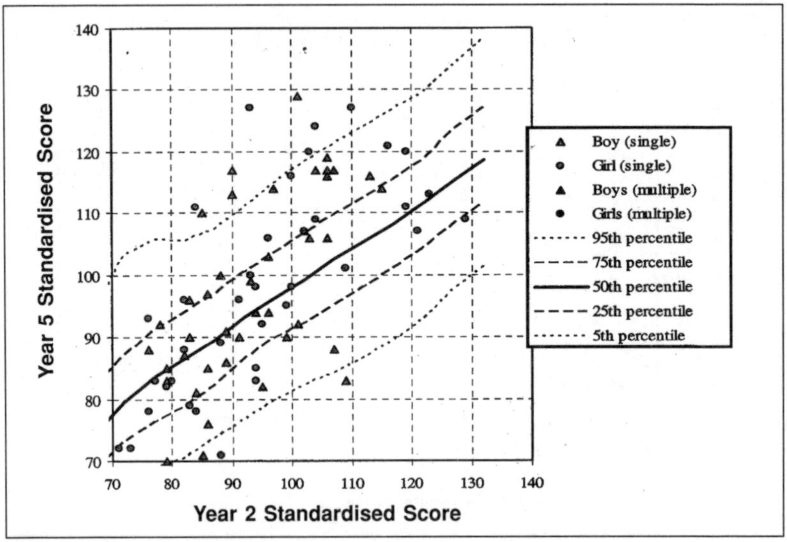

Figure 13.3: Pupils' Year 5 standardised scores in relation to their Year 2 standardised scores in Maltese.

nationally. Since the number of pupils within a particular category can be quite small, these comparisons had to be treated with caution. However, this exercise is important to help schools to identify which groups of pupils are doing well and which groups may need further attention.

Table 13.4 is the same as Table 13.3 but deals with the Maltese test result scores. The table provides a school mean (or average) and the national mean for a range of background variables. This enables the school to see whether its pupils (with particular background characteristics) have done better than expected in Maltese compared with pupils nationally.

Figures 13.4 and 13.5 enable the school to look at the overall distribution of its Year 5 pupils' standardised scores when compared with national standardised scores for English and Maltese. The school's scores are represented by bars, and the national standardised scores by black dots.

Table 13.3: English Year 5 Standardised Scores by Pupil Background Variables

Variable		Number	School Mean	National Mean
Sex	Boy	55	89.8	98.9
	Girl	43	92.3	101.1
Age	Up to 9:7	34	92.3	100.4
	Over 9:7	65	90.3	99.7
SEN	None	96	91.5	101.0
	Mild to moderate SEN	1	74.0	88.5
	Severe to very severe SEN	2	72.0	84.5
First Language	Maltese	99	90.9	99.1
	English	0	–	111.1
	Other	0	–	99.0
Father's Occupation	Professional	2	102.0	110.9
	Administrative	6	97.8	108.3
	Clerical	10	95.2	102.8
	Skilled	38	94.1	96.9
	Semi-, un-skilled	28	86.5	94.4
	Other	15	84.1	91.4
Mother's Occupation	Professional	0	–	110.3
	Administrative	0	–	111.2
	Clerical	2	100.0	107.5
	Skilled	1	81.0	101.2
	Semi-, un-skilled	6	87.2	94.8
	Other	89	91.1	98.4
Father's Education	No formal schooling	3	79.7	91.6
	Primary school	19	87.8	92.5
	Secondary school	53	91.1	98.8
	Pre-university & vocational courses	7	106.6	107.2
	University Education	4	103.5	110.4
	Other	13	85.2	87.9
Mother's Education	No formal schooling	3	80.0	91.2
	Primary school	10	80.7	90.9
	Secondary school	72	92.3	99.1
	Pre-university & vocational courses	7	104.0	109.4
	University Education	1	97.0	111.3
	Other	6	81.5	85.5

Table 13.4: Maltese Year 5 Standardised Scores by Pupil Background Variables

Variable		Number	School Mean	National Mean
Sex	Boy	55	92.5	98.4
	Girl	43	95.7	101.4
Age	Up to 9:7	33	98.2	100.2
	Over 9:7	66	92.0	99.6
SEN	None	96	94.8	100.9
	Mild to moderate SEN	1	69.0	85.8
	Severe to very severe SEN	2	73.5	81.4
First Language	Maltese	99	94.1	100.2
	English	0	–	96.9
	Other	0	–	92.1
Father's Occupation	Professional	2	110.0	105.8
	Administrative	6	103.2	103.5
	Clerical	10	95.8	103.9
	Skilled	38	98.4	98.8
	Semi-, un-skilled	28	88.5	96.4
	Other	15	86.7	92.5
Mother's Occupation	Professional	0	–	106.4
	Administrative	0	–	100.3
	Clerical	2	103.0	105.8
	Skilled	1	78.0	101.7
	Semi-, un-skilled	6	81.8	96.1
	Other	89	94.7	99.3
Father's Education	No formal schooling	3	87.0	94.1
	Primary school	19	90.3	94.6
	Secondary school	53	93.8	100.0
	Pre-university & vocational courses	7	113.6	104.2
	University Education	4	109.3	106.0
	Other	13	87.5	88.1
Mother's Education	No formal schooling	3	99.3	93.8
	Primary school	10	82.5	92.8
	Secondary school	72	94.1	100.1
	Pre-university & vocational courses	7	111.3	105.0
	University Education	1	117.0	106.0
	Other	6	87.2	87.6

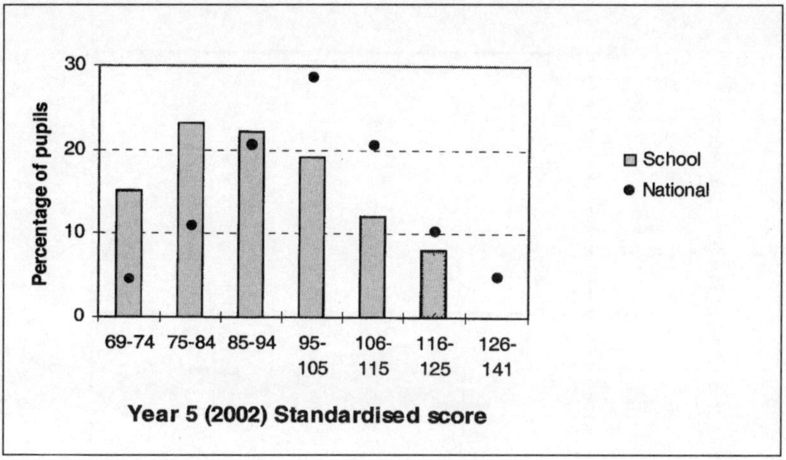

Figure 13.4: Distribution of standardised scores achieved in English.

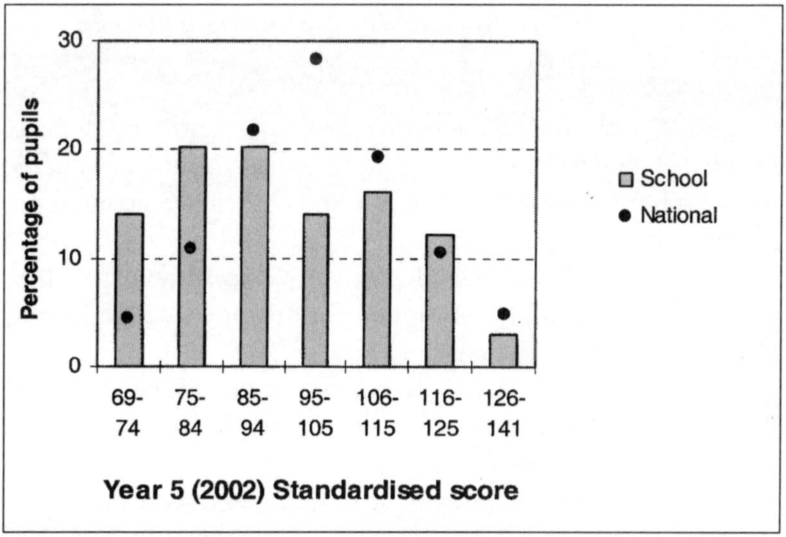

Figure 13.5: Distribution of standardised scores achieved in Maltese.

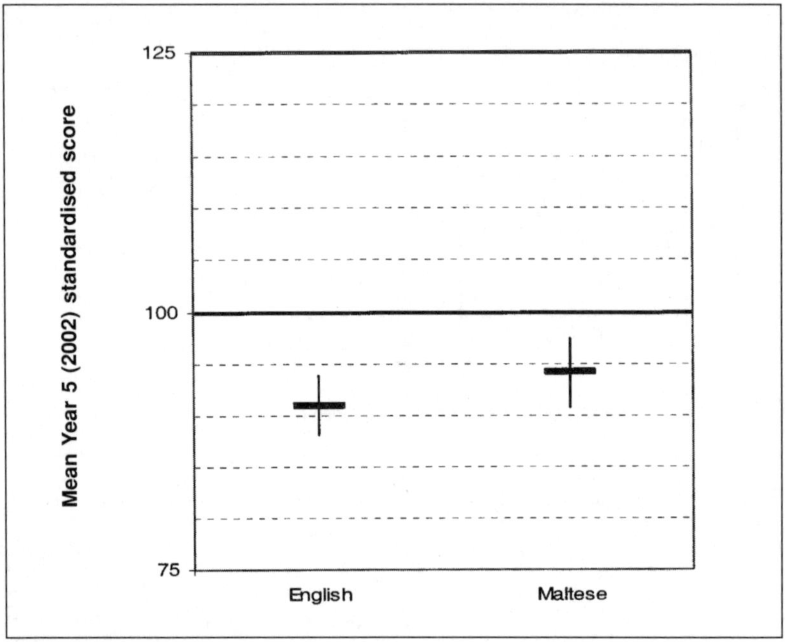

Figure 13.6: School mean standardised scores with 95% confidence intervals.

Figure 13.6 shows the mean (average) age-standardised scores for English and Maltese for the pupils who took the tests in the model school reported here. It also indicates a '95% confidence interval' for each mean score.

If any vertical line is wholly above the horizontal '100' line, then one may say that performance in that area is significantly above the national average.

If any vertical line is wholly below the horizontal '100' line, then performance in that area is significantly below the national average for the subject.

Figure 13.6 shows mean (average) standardised scores in English and Maltese for Year 5 pupils. It provides a clear illustration of the school's mean scores in relation to the national mean standardised score of 100. The vertical line through each of the

English and Maltese standardised scores enables the school to see whether performance in each subject is 'statistically significant'. In this case, a close look at Figure 13.6 shows that this particular school is below the national average in both subjects, since the vertical lines are wholly below the horizontal '100' line.

Figure 13.7 shows the average change in age-standardised scores between Year 2 and Year 5 for English and Maltese. It also indicates a '95% confidence interval' for each change in age-standardised scores.

If any vertical line is wholly above the horizontal '0' line, then one may say that change in age-standardised scores in that area is significantly above zero, indicating that more progress has been made than would have been expected.

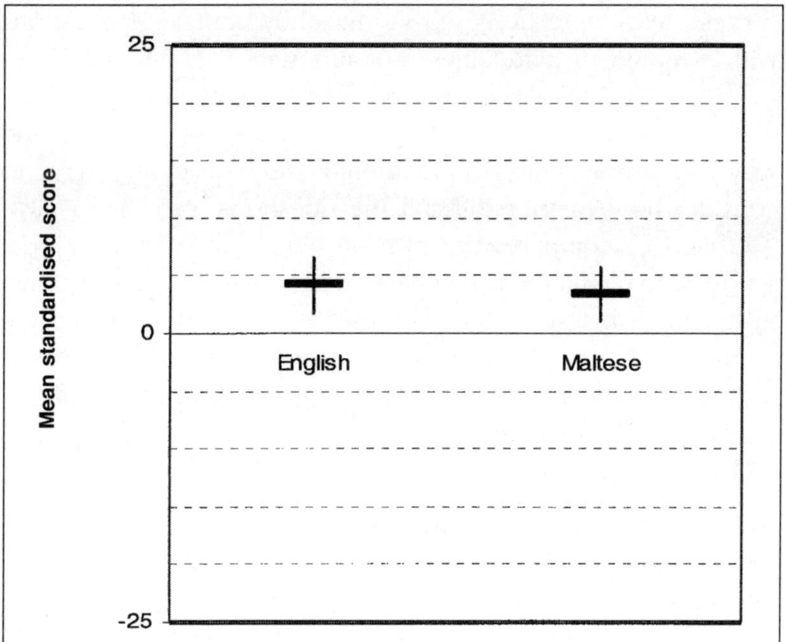

Figure 13.7: School mean changes in standardised scores from Year 2 to Year 5, with 95% confidence intervals.

If any vertical line is wholly below the horizontal '0' line, then one may say that change in age-standardised scores in that area is significantly below zero, indicating that progress has been less than might be expected.

Figure 13.7 is similar to Figure 13.6, but shows the average changes in standardised scores over the three-year period from Year 2 to Year 5. This is the amount of progress made by the pupils in the particular school.

13.3 Item Facilities Report

Tables 13.5 and 13.6 are item facility reports for the Year 5 English and Maltese tests. Each question (or item) on each test is listed, along with the facility, which is the percentage of pupils who got that particular question correct.

These tests were designed so that they contained questions with a range of difficulties. So although it is of interest to consider which questions the pupils in a particular school did well on, with high percentages giving correct answers, and which questions they found difficult, it is also important to consider how easy or difficult the questions were nationally.

Table 13.5 compares the pupils' performance of the model school with the national averages for particular questions (items) in the English test. The questions are arranged such that the items on which pupils performed better than the national average appear first and items that pupils found more difficult appear lower down the list.

The questions were categorised according to:

the type of text they relate to

- narrative
- non-narrative

the skills required in the response/answer

- retrieval skills
- inference skills

Table 13.5: Year 5 Item Facilities Report for English

Text Type	Question Type		Description	School (%)	National (%)	School – National Difference (%)
NN	I	Q25	True or False: The rainforest is not a safe home for parrots	49	42	7
NN	R	Q28	True or False: Some farmers think parrots are a nuisance	33	28	5
N	I	Q8	Who might have said: He doesn't need a cage	76	77	–1
N	R	Q15	Should or Should Not Do: Avoid eating unripe plums	39	41	–2
N	I	Q7	Who shouted at the bush?	55	59	–4
NN	I	Q34	Missing Word: listening	4	8	–4
NN	I	Q33	Missing Word: about	1	5	–4
NN	R	Q23	True or False: People will pay a great deal of money for a pet parrot	47	51	–4
NN	I	Q19	Where does the kakapo live?	33	38	–5
NN	I	Q26	True or False: Kakapos think they can fly	42	47	–5
NN	R	Q22	True or False: Kakapos cannot climb trees	40	46	–6
N	I	Q13	Should or Should Not Do: Get up after sunrise	45	51	–6
NN	R	Q27	True or False: Most parrots that get trapped end up in cages in Europe or North America	60	66	–6
NN	I	Q30	Missing Word: able/known	0	8	–8
NN	I	Q41	Which of these might be called *Things Every Parrot Should Know?*	42	50	–8
N	I	Q9	Who might have said: He'll spoil the carpet	71	79	–8
N	I	Q17	Should or Should Not Do: Drink water from the river	64	73	–9
NN	I	Q38	Which of these is most likely to be about something which could really happen?	49	58	–9
NN	R	Q29	True or False: Parrots only use their beaks to crack nuts or roots	28	37	–9
NN	I	Q36	Missing Word: telling	8	17	–9

Table 13.5: Year 5 Item Facilities Report for English (continued)

Text Type	Question Type		Description	School (%)	National (%)	School – National Difference (%)
NN	I	Q35	Missing Word: began/started/learned	11	20	–9
N	I	Q12	Who might have said: At least he doesn't tell me what to do	45	54	–9
NN	I	Q24	True or False: Parrots come in all different colours	69	78	–9
NN	I	Q39	Which of these would give you the most useful information for a project on *Birds of the Rainforest*?	68	78	–10
NN	I	Q21	Which of the following things can you learn about the person who wrote *Parrots in Danger*?	42	52	–10
NN	R	Q1	Things that fly: Kite	82	93	–11
N	I	Q11	Who might have said: I loves Granda! I loves Granda!	73	85	–12
NN	I	Q37	Missing Word: do	12	24	–12
N	I	Q16	Should or Should Not Do: Stay awake until midnight	48	60	–12
NN	I	Q31	Missing Word: talk/communicate	27	40	–13
NN	I	Q40	Which of these might be called *A Family Disagreement*?	34	49	–15
NN	I	Q32	Missing Word: birds/animals/creatures	12	27	–15
N	I	Q5	Who shouted at the shed?	60	77	–17
NN	R	Q20	Where did the earliest known parrot live?	49	66	–17
N	I	Q14	Should or Should Not Do: Argue with a hornbill	43	61	–18
NN	R	Q3	Things that fly: Arrow	70	88	–18
NN	R	Q18	Which of these birds is the largest?	57	76	–19
N	I	Q6	Who shouted back?	48	70	–22
NN	R	Q4	Things that fly: Pigeon	59	82	–23
N	I	Q10	Who might have said: That parrot has pecked all the apples I brought you	55	79	–24
NN	R	Q2	Things that fly: Crow	29	61	–32

Text Type: N – Narrative; NN – Non-Narrative
Question Type: R – Retrieval; I – Inference

Table 13.6: Year 5 Item Facilities Report for Maltese

Text Type	Question Type		Description	School (%)	National (%)	School – National Difference (%)
NN	I	Q28	Veru jew le: Xi bdiewa jqisu lill-pappagalli bħala biċċa uġigħ ta' ras	30	22	8
N	R	Q13	X'għandhom jagħmlu jew ma jagħmlux: Iqumu wara tlugħ ix-xemx	58	54	4
NN	I	Q25	Veru jew le: Ir-rainforest mhix post ta' kenn għall-pappagalli	31	30	1
NN	R	Q2	Affarijiet li jtiru: Naħla	90	89	1
NN	I	Q40	Liema waħda minn dawn seta' kien jisimha *Nuqqas ta' qbil fil-familja?*	58	59	–1
N	I	Q7	Min kien ħemm fis-siġra tar-rand?	66	67	–1
NN	I	Q26	Veru jew le: Il-kakapos jaħsbu li jafu jtiru	47	49	–2
NN	I	Q41	Liema waħda minn dawn seta' kien jisimha *Ħwejjeġ li kull pappagall jeħtieġ ikun jaf?*	48	51	–3
NN	I	Q24	Veru jew le: Il-pappagalli għandhom ħafna kuluri differenti	83	86	–3
N	R	Q15	X'għandhom jagħmlu jew ma jagħmlux: Ma jiklux frott nej	35	38	–3
NN	R	Q1	Affarijiet li jtiru: Tajra	92	97	–5
NN	I	Q30	Kelma nieqsa: jafu/kapaċi	28	33	–5
NN	I	Q31	Kelma nieqsa: jitkellem/jitħaddet	42	47	–5
NN	I	Q33	Kelma nieqsa: ħila/kapaċità	2	7	–5
N	I	Q5	Min għajjat lejn il-kmajra?	78	84	–6
NN	R	Q3	Affarijiet li jtiru: Ajruplan	90	96	–6
NN	I	Q19	Fejn jgħix il-kakapo?	28	34	–6
NN	I	Q38	Liema waħda minn dawn, hija dwar ħaġa li l-aktar tista' tiġri tassew?	51	58	–7
NN	I	Q37	Kelma nieqsa: jobdi/jagħmel	42	49	–7
NN	I	Q34	Kelma nieqsa: tgħallmu	12	19	–7
NN	R	Q4	Affarijiet li jtiru: Merill	86	93	–7
NN	R	Q27	Veru jew le: Ħafna mill-pappagalli li jinqabdu jispiċċaw f'gaġġa fl-Ewropa jew fl-Amerika ta' Fuq	56	64	–8

Table 13.6: Year 5 Item Facilities Report for Maltese (continued)

Text Type	Question Type		Description	School (%)	National (%)	School-National Difference (%)
NN	R	Q29	Veru jew le: Il-pappagalli jużaw munqarhom biss biex ikissru l-lewż u jħaffru għall-għeruq	27	35	– 8
NN	I	Q32	Kelma nieqsa: annimali/ħlejjaq/kreaturi	18	26	– 8
N	I	Q17	X'għandhom jagħmlu jew ma jagħmlux: Jixorbu l-ilma mix-xmara	70	78	– 8
N	R	Q14	X'għandhom jagħmlu jew ma jagħmlux: Imieru lill-hornbill	65	74	– 9
NN	I	Q39	Liema waħda minn dawn tista' tagħtik informazzjoni l-aktar siewja għal proġett dwar *L-Għasafar tar-rainforest*?	74	83	– 9
NN	I	Q21	Minn dak li qrajt, x'sirt taf dwar il-persuna li kitbet *Pappagalli fil-periklu*?	47	56	– 9
N	I	Q10	Min seta' qal: Dak il-pappagall naqqar it-tuffieħ kollu li ġibtlek	72	81	– 9
NN	R	Q20	Fejn kienu jgħixu l-ewwel pappagalli li nafu bihom?	66	76	–10
N	I	Q12	Min seta' qal: Ta' lanqas hu ma joqgħodx jgħidli x'għandi nagħmel	51	61	–10
NN	I	Q35	Kelma nieqsa: tgħallem/dera	13	23	–10
N	I	Q11	Min seta' qal: Inħobbu lin-nannu. Inħobbu lin-nannu	79	90	–11
N	I	Q8	Min seta' qal: M'għandux bżonn gaġġa	70	81	–11
N	I	Q6	Min wieġeb lura?	63	75	–12
NN	I	Q36	Kelma nieqsa: jgħid/isejjaħ/jikkmanda/jordna	16	28	–12
NN	I	Q23	Veru jew le: In-nies iħallsu ħafna flus biex ikollhom pappaġall bħala pet	41	53	–12
N	I	Q9	Min seta' qal: Tapit ġdid se jaħlih	67	80	–13
NN	R	Q18	Min hu l-ikbar minn dawn l-għasafar?	65	78	–13
N	I	Q16	X'għandhom jagħmlu jew ma jagħmlux: Jibqgħu mqajmin sa nofs il-lejl	52	66	–14
NN	R	Q22	Veru jew le: Il-kakapos ma jistgħux jixxabtu ma' siġar	32	48	–16

Text Type: N – Narrative; NN – Non-Narrative
Question Type: R – Retrieval; I – Inference

This means that, as well as looking at individual questions, the school can compare the performance of its pupils for Narrative (N) items and Non-Narrative (NN) items; for Retrieval (R) skills and Inference (I) skills. This should help the schools to identify strengths and weaknesses in the performance of their pupils.

Schools could, for example, consider the most positive responses (at the top of the list) and the most negative responses. In relation to questions where pupils have not performed particularly well, the school might want to focus more on that type of question format to help its pupils to improve.

Chapter 14

Feedback Provided to Schools

Schools were guided about how their individual report can be put into practical use. Thus, in addition to a thorough discussion with every school on their individual school report, training was provided to heads of schools on how policy makers, schools, parents, teachers and pupils can work together for school improvement in general. Schools and advisors together were asked to investigate the performance of different groups of pupils, and to focus particularly on groups that the school was not reaching. Schools were asked to self-evaluate their current practices as objectively as possible and to investigate the areas that need to be highlighted for improvement. It was also important for schools to identify their areas of success in order to be able to share these with other schools.

The training was organised in three main parts:

Part 1: Principles of using value added data for school improvement
Part 2: What does this mean for the individual school?
Part 3: Strategies for addressing underachievement

14.1 Principles of Using Value Added Data for School Improvement

The school's value added report is based upon a number of principles. These can be expressed as follows:

- Schools make a difference – schools need good quantitative information about their pupils' performance and progress, relative to other schools, for long-term strategic planning purposes.
- As far as possible, value added data should take account

of individual pupils' prior attainment together with other factors known to affect performance, such as parents' occupational background.

- The analysis should be confidential to the school so that the data they supply is not used for any other purpose than to feed back evidence about how well their pupils have done.
- Quantitative data about academic performance reflects only one aspect of what schools do: such data should not override other aspects, e.g. school ethos, in helping to decide whether or not a school is 'effective'. Teachers have detailed professional knowledge of their pupils and the data should be used in the context of this professional knowledge.
- Quantitative data provides only one instrument of evaluation; it reveals correlations, not causes. It needs to be used with caution and alongside qualitative data in a complementary way, to raise further questions and to inform longer-term school improvement strategies.
- There is now a consensus that an important factor in achieving school improvement is a culture of self-evaluation at the institutional, departmental and classroom levels. This means that schools, and teachers within schools, need to 'own' the data and find appropriate ways of utilising it in their own context to generate action plans.

14.2 Questions the School Needs to Ask for Self-evaluation

Schools were presented with the following questions, which their individualised school profile may help them to answer about their individual school.

- How is your school currently performing?
- What are the main differences between scores in English and Maltese?

- What are the possible reasons for these differences?
- Have some groups of pupils performed better than others? If so, in what ways?
- Are there any differences in boys' and girls' performance? If so, what are the possible reasons for these differences?
- How does the school's performance compare with other schools' performance?
- Have your teachers' expectations of their students been appropriate?
- Have pupils made the progress they should have made?

14.3 Strategies for Addressing Underachievement

One of the major concerns of schools is how to deal with underachievement. Schools were presented with the following points for reflection on the subject. Underachievement was discussed focusing mainly on four main aspects:

- pupil groups
- teaching and learning styles
- curriculum and resources
- assessment

14.3.1 Strategies for Addressing Underachievement in Relation to Pupil Groups

- Do boys or girls need particular attention?
- Do any particular year groups or age ranges need attention?
- Do any particular ability ranges (high, medium or low) need attention?
- Is there a need for more differentiation, and adapting to pupil abilities?
- Would it be worth looking at grouping, setting or streaming arrangements?
- Are there any disaffected or poorly-motivated pupils? What could the school do about this?

14.3.2 Strategies for Addressing Underachievement by Using Effective Teaching and Learning Styles

- It is imperative to have an audit of teaching strategies across the school, departments, year groups.
- What are the strengths in the school's teaching and learning strategies?
- What are the weaknesses in the school's teaching and learning strategies?
- Does the school need to look at teachers' pace, variety, structure and clarity?
- Do teachers share information? Would peer lesson observation help?
- Would pupils benefit from work on "thinking skills"?
- Are pupils being given appropriate thinking time?
- Are teacher, pupil and parent expectations high enough?
- Are there any areas where more training and professional development is required?

14.3.3 Strategies for Addressing Underachievement Using an Appropriate Curriculum and Resources

- Which particular subjects or departments are the most successful? Why?
- One can look at the progress of one individual across several subjects. Why the differences?
- Are the syllabi or modules within syllabi appropriate?
- What learning support strategies could be used?
- Is it worth trying mentoring, use of learning support assistants or extra tuition?
- Is more revision time or are extra lessons required?

14.3.4 Strategies for Addressing Underachievement through Proper Assessment

- Is the reporting, monitoring and assessment system doing all it should be?
- Is there enough diagnostic work going on (as opposed to monitoring)?
- Is the setting of work done consistently?
- What types of questions or tests do pupils do less well at?
- Is marking done consistently and at the appropriate levels?
- Is the school giving enough positive feedback to its pupils? Is there a merit system?
- Is there appropriate target setting? Is it challenging and realistic?
- Who should be setting targets? Subjects, departments, teachers or pupils?
- Do pupils have enough understanding and involvement in target setting?

Through such a process of self-evaluation schools can engage in forward planning which has clearly identified objectives and areas for further development. In this way schools can ensure that they are adding value to their pupils' education and equipping **all** their pupils with the essential skills required for them to be able to meet the life challenges which lie ahead of them.

Annex I

Technical Glossary of the Statistical Terms used in the Individual School Report

Adjusted

Where given characteristics have been included in a statistical model, we say that the results have been adjusted for these characteristics. This means that schools (and/or pupils) are compared on like-with-like basis.

Correlation

A correlation is a measure of the strength of the relationship (which is not necessarily causal) between two quantities. Correlations have values in the range +1 to -1. A value of +1 indicates a direct positive relationship, whereas a value of -1 indicates a direct negative relationship, and 0 indicates no relationship all. Correlations based on fewer than 1000 cases should be treated with caution.

Mean Score

This is another term for the average score.

Median and Percentiles

The median is the mid-point of an ordered set of data. The median divides the observations (in this case, pupils) into two equal parts. The median line is such that 50 per cent of the observations lie above it and 50 per cent lie below it. For this reason the median line is also called the 50th percentile.

It is additionally possible to draw a line that divides the set of data such that 25 per cent of the observations lie below the line and 75 per cent lie above, namely the lower quartile or 25th percentile. The 5th, 75th and 95th percentiles are constructed similarly.

Multilevel Modelling

Multilevel modelling is a particular type of statistical model, which takes account of data which is grouped into similar clusters at different levels. In this report individual pupils are grouped within schools. Also, pupils have been tested at two time points. There may be more in common between pupils within the same school than with other schools, and there may be elements of similarity between the school's test results at different time points. Multilevel modelling allows us to take account of this hierarchical structure of the data and variables at the different levels so as to produce more accurate predictions, as well as estimates of the differences from Year 2 to Year 5, between pupils and between schools.

'Predicted' or Expected Value

The predicted value is the value given by a statistical model at any specified point. It represents the performance of a 'typical' school or pupil with a given set of characteristics.

Raw Score

This is the number of marks obtained by a pupil in a test. A raw score on one test is not comparable to a raw score on another test. This is because the tests may be of different length or difficulty. A raw score does not include any allowance for a pupil's age.

Residual

A residual is the difference between one school's (or pupil's) actual value and the 'predicted' value.

Scatterplot

When relationships between two measures on the same set of objects are to be investigated, it is often useful to plot them on a graph with one measure on the X-axis and the other on the Y-axis. Each object or individual then appears as a point on the graph, and relationships can be seen quite easily.

Standardised Score

This is the pupil's raw score put onto a different scale. Using a common scale means that standardised scores from one test can be compared with standardised scores from another test. Also, an age-allowance is included which means that pupils of different ages can be compared.

Statistically, the 'average' standardised score is 100. A higher score is above 'average' and a score below 100 is below 'average'. About two thirds of pupils will have standardised scores between 85 and 115.

The minimum age-standardised score for the tests used for this evaluation is 69 and the maximum is 131.

Statistical Model

A statistical model specifies the relationship between one measure (e.g. prior attainment) and another (e.g. total Year 5 score), which is related to it. A statistical model then represents the average or expected relationship for a group of schools or pupils.

Statistical Significance

We say that there is a statistically significant difference between two groups in some quantity if the probability of that difference arising by chance, i.e. if there were no real difference, is less than a preset value (usually five per cent).

Upper and Lower limit

No statistical estimate is ever totally accurate, but the degree of accuracy will depend on a number of factors, including the amount of data on which it is based. To indicate the degree of inaccuracy we compute a confidence interval, commonly 95 per cent. This represents the range of values within which there is a 95% probability that the 'true value' lies. The upper and lower limits define this range. Thus, a 95% confidence interval with an upper limit of 98 and a lower limit of 93 for the average score would mean that there is a 95% chance that the true average is above 93 and below 98.

References

BARTOLO, P. (1988). *Report on Maltese Word-Reading Test.* Malta: Education Department.

BROOKS, G., GORMAN, T.P., HARMAN, J., HUTCHISON, D. and WILKIN, A. (1996). *Family Literacy Works: the NFER Evaluation of the Basic Skills Agency's Family Literacy Demonstration Programmes,* London: Basic Skills Agency.

BROOKS, G., GORMAN, T.P., HARMAN, J., HUTCHISON, D., KINDER, K., MOOR, H. and WILKIN, A. (1997). *Family Literacy Lasts: the NFER Follow-up Study of the Basic Skills Agency's Demonstration Programmes,* London: Basic Skills Agency.

BROOKS, G. (2003). *What Works for Children with Literacy Difficulties? The effectiveness of intervention schemes,* Department for Education and Skills, Research Report 380. London: Department for Education and Skills.

DAVIES, J., HALLAM, S. and IRESON, J. (2003). Ability groupings in the primary school: issues arising from practice, *Research Papers in Education*, Vol. 18, No. 1 pp. 45-60.

FALZON, J. (1972). *Maltese Group Reading Test.* Malta: Education Department.

GOLDSTEIN, H. (2003). *Multilevel Statistical Models: Third Edition* (Kendall's Library of Statistics 3). London: Arnold.

HUTCHISON, D. (1993). School effectiveness studies using administrative data, *Educational Research*, Vol. 35, pp. 27-47.

HUTCHISON, D. (2003). The Effect of Group-level Influences on Pupils' Progress in Reading, *British Education Research Journal*, Vol. 29, No. 1, pp. 25-39.

KENNY, D.A. (1975). A quasi-experimental approach to assessing treatment effects in the non-equivalent control group design, *Psychological Bull.,* Vol. 82, pp. 345-362.

MARTINELLI, V.C. (1996). *Early metalinguistic abilities and subsequent reading and spelling achievements of Maltese children.* Unpublished PhD thesis, University of Manchester, UK.

MIFSUD, C.L., MILTON, J., BROOKS, G. and HUTCHISON, D. (2000). *Literacy in Malta: The 1999 National Survey of Attainment of Year 2 Pupils.* Slough: NFER and the University of Malta.

MULLIS, I.V.S., MARTIN, M.O., GONZALEZ, E.J. and KENNEDY, A.M. (2003). *PIRLS 2001 International Report: IEA's Study of Reading Literacy Achievement in Primary School in 35 Countries.* Boston, MA: Boston College, International Study Centre.

OPDENAKKER, M. and VAN DAMME, J. (2001) Relationship between School Composition and Characteristics of School Process and their Effect on Mathematics Achievement, *British Education Research Journal,* Vol. 27, No. 4, pp. 407-431.

RASBASH, J., GOLDSTEIN, H., BROWNE, W.J., YANG, M. and WOODHOUSE, G. (2000). *The MLwiN command interface (Version 1.3).*

RAUDENBUSH, S.W. and BRYK, A.S. (2002). *Hierarchical Linear Models: second edition.* Newbury Park: Sage.

SCHAGEN, I. and MORRISON, J. (1998). *QUASE Overview Report 1997.* Slough: NFER.

SCHAGEN, I. & GOLDSTEIN, H. (2002). Do Specialist Schools Add Value? – Some methodological problems, *Research Intelligence,* No. 80, pp. 12-15.

STRAND, S. (1997). Pupil Progress during Key Stage 1: a value added analysis of school effects, *British Education Research Journal,* Vol. 23, No. 4, pp. 471-487.

STRAND, S. (1999). Ethnic Group, Sex and Economic Disadvantage: associations with pupils' educational progress from Baseline to the end of Key Stage 1, *British Education Research Journal*, Vol. 25, No. 2, pp. 179-202.

STRAND, S. (2002). Pupil Mobility, Attainment and Progress During Key Stage 1: a study in cautious interpretation, *British Education Research Journal*, Vol. 28, No. 1, pp. 63-78.

THRUPP, M. (2001). Recent School Effectiveness Counter-critiques: problems and possibilities, *British Education Research Journal*, Vol. 27, No. 4, pp. 443-457.

TYMMS, P., MERRELL, C. and HENDERSON, B. (1997). The First Year at School: A Quantitative Investigation of the Attainment and Progress of Pupils, *Educational Research and Evaluation*, Vol.3, No.2, pp. 101-118.

VASSALLO, M., FARRUGIA SANT'ANGELO, V. and SCIRIHA, L. (1994). *Too Late for Too Many – A Study of Special Education in Malta.* Malta: Media Centre.

VINCENT, D., CRUMPLER, M. and DE LA MARE, M. (1996). *Reading Progress Test 3.* London: Hodder and Stoughton Ltd.

VINCENT, D., CRUMPLER, M. and DE LA MARE, M. (1997). *Manual for Stage Two of the Reading Progress Tests (for use with Reading Progress Tests 3 to 6).* London: Hodder and Stoughton Ltd.

Author Index

Subject Index